Turtle Island

THE STORY OF NORTH AMERICA'S FIRST PEOPLE

ELDON YELLOWHORN & KATHY LOWINGER

annick press
toronto + berkeley

To Presley & Jezebelle —EY
For Pat –KL

With thanks to Rivka Cranley, designer Tania Craan, and all the Annick staff. My deepest appreciation to Pat Malis, Reena Kronitz, Mike Naymark, and especially to Bill Harnum for reading several drafts. And to Chandra Wohleber for her sensitive, patient, and careful editing, my gratitude. –KL

© 2017 Eldon Yellowhorn
and Kathy Lowinger (text)
Ninth printing, December 2023
Cover art/design by Tania Craan
Designed by Tania Craan
Photo Research: MacCap Permissions

Annick Press Ltd.

We acknowledge the support of the Canada Council for the Arts and the Ontario Arts Council, and the participation of the Government of Canada/la participation du gouvernement du Canada for our publishing activities.

Cataloging in Publication
Yellowhorn, Eldon, 1956-, author
    Turtle Island : the story of North America's
    first people / Eldon Yellowhorn
    & Kathy Lowinger.
Includes bibliographical references and index.
Issued in print and electronic formats.
ISBN 978-1-55451-944-6 (hardcover).
ISBN 978-1-55451-943-9 (softcover).
ISBN 978-1-55451-945-3 (EPUB).
ISBN 978-1-55451-946-0 (PDF)
    1. Indians of North America--History.
    I. Lowinger, Kathy, author II. Title.
E77.Y35 2017   970.004'97
C2017-901706-3
    C2017-901707-1

Published in the U.S.A. by Annick Press (U.S.) Ltd.
Distributed in Canada by
    University of Toronto Press.
Distributed in the U.S.A. by
    Publishers Group West.

Printed in China
Visit us at: www.annickpress.com

CONTENTS

A Glimpse into the Past 4

The Beginning
Turtle Island 6

Chapter 1
Finding Our Way
to the Past 9

Chapter 2
North America in
the Days of Ice 15

Chapter 3
Listening to the Land 29

Chapter 4
Ideas Spread 43

Chapter 5
Change-Makers 55

Chapter 6
First Contact 67

Chapter 7
In the Year 1491 75

Chapter 8
After the End
of the World 87

Chapter 9
Healing the Circle 101

Selected Sources 109

Further Reading 110

Image Credits 111

Index 113

A Glimpse into the Past

THIS IS AN UNUSUAL KIND of history book. Many people lived on this land from the beginning of human history to 1491. We could not possibly do justice to the stories of all those people, but we will give you a glimpse into their fascinating past, rich with accomplishment and tradition.

This isn't the kind of history where one event leads to another along a straight line. We do follow a time line of sorts—from the Ice Age to 1491, with concluding chapters that bring us up to the present. In between, the dates are only a rough guide, and—before 1491—are all approximate unless otherwise noted. In places, we tell the story through myths, and we don't ascribe even rough dates for those. Instead of telling Turtle Island's story through dates, we look at what life was like in different places across North America to celebrate the wisdom and ingenuity of the people.

Another thing you'll find unusual about this book is the lack of names. That goes for individuals, groups, and places. We simply don't have names to attach to the engineers who built Cahokia or the artists who painted the images in the Lower Pecos or the inventors of the ovens that turned a poisonous plant into something good to eat. We aren't always sure what people called themselves, the groups they lived in, their neighbors, or their land. Names are very powerful, so instead of misusing them, we have steered away when we could. However, you will see the names of several archaeologists because we do know who they are.

There was no such thing as Canada, the United States, or Mexico. The borders we know today didn't exist, but to help you find your way, we've used current names of places.

The most important name is what to call the people who are the subject of this book. You've probably heard different ways to describe the original people of North America: Indian, Aboriginal, First Nations, Native Americans. We're using the word *Indigenous*, with some exceptions. When we refer to the Indian Act, the Bureau of Indian Affairs, and other government-related terms, we use *Indian* to avoid confusion.

Finally, an important note about the human remains that have helped unlock the story of Turtle Island. Much of what we know is thanks to the study of human bones and teeth. Over the years, the skeletons of Indigenous people have been dug up not only for study by archaeologists but also accidentally by construction workers, or for profit by grave robbers. Human remains deserve to be treated with the highest respect, and that has often not happened.

When the colony of British Columbia passed the Indian Graves Ordinance in 1865, it was the first public law to ban grave robbing, and it made all Indigenous cemeteries government property. In the United States, the Antiquities Act of 1906 declared that all Indian bones and artifacts on federal land belonged to the United States. Eighty-four years later, in 1990, the government of the United States finally passed the Native American Graves Protection and Repatriation Act, which requires that all human remains, burial objects, and other sacred objects be returned to descendants' communities for reburial. We acknowledge the great debt we owe to the ancestors, and to their descendants.

The Beginning
Turtle Island

FROM THE **HAUDENOSAUNEE TRADITION**

The Story of Sky Woman

Long before the world was created, there was an island in the sky where the Sky People lived. One day, a tree toppled over and tore a hole in the sky. A pregnant Sky Woman grew curious about the hole. She came near—so near that she tumbled through the opening. She grabbed at tobacco and strawberry plants, but they didn't stop her fall. She was still clutching the tobacco and strawberries when a flock of birds swooped to catch her.

The birds set her down on the Great Turtle's back. Other animals dove to the ocean floor and brought mud up to the surface. They packed the mud on the Great Turtle's back. Over and over, they dove down until they had brought up enough mud to make room for trees and plants to grow. Then they dove some more. When they were finished, they had made a whole world on the Great Turtle's back. Sky Woman gave birth, and when she did she became the mother of the people. The land has been called Turtle Island ever since.

THE HAUDENOSAUNEE, who live around the Great Lakes, have told Sky Woman's story for countless generations. Turtle Island is what they call the land that was created thanks to Sky Woman and the Great Turtle. Of course, many other groups of people have lived in North America, each of them with their own name for their home.

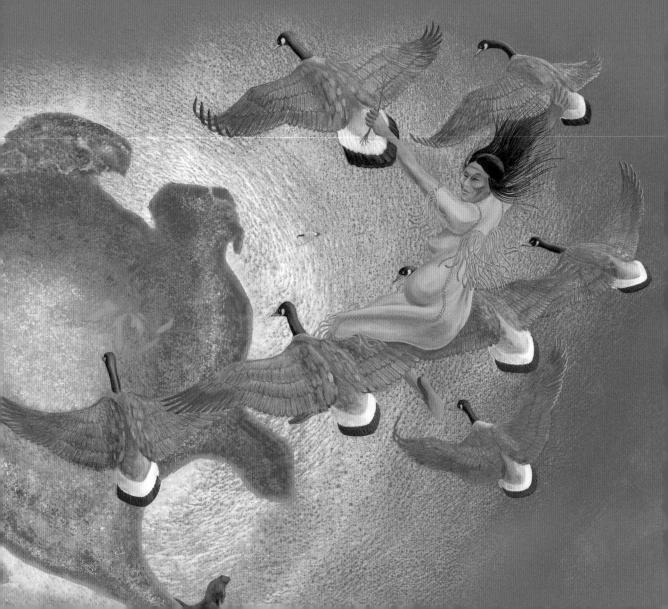

Chapter 1

Finding Our Way to the Past

THE WAY TO TURTLE ISLAND

★ The Story Myths Tell

★ The Story Science Tells

★ The Story Your Imagination Tells

★ Together, they are a path that takes us into the past

THE STORY MYTHS TELL

Even though thousands of years have gone by, we have ways to step back into the past. One way is by listening to ancient myths, or traditional stories, that are handed down from one generation to another. Writing and papermaking were not traditions among the peoples of North America. Instead, the past is captured in myths, preserved for us thanks to memory and storytelling.

Some myths are based on facts, some tell about the deeds of gods and heroes, and some describe rituals. Creation myths such as the story of Sky Woman tell how the world came to be. Others explain what happens to us after we die. And still others tell us how we should behave during the time in between. Whether they are funny, frightening, or full of information, myths are sacred to the people who tell them, listen to them, and pass them on. Myths don't just belong to the past—Indigenous people still tell the ancient stories because they value their spoken traditions as a vital way to understand history.

For instance, geologists know that earthquakes were common in the past. We know the exact date in late January 1700 when the last great earthquake shook the West Coast. The tsunami it generated was even recorded in Japan. Perhaps it also inspired the story "Thunderbird and Whale."

Bill Reid's *Raven and the First Men* was carved from a giant block of yellow cedar. In Haida myth, Raven found a clamshell on the seashore, with tiny people emerging from it. He coaxed them out so that they could share in the wonderful world.

Thunderbird and Whale

Thunderbird and Whale were gigantic. Whale was so enormous that every living thing in the world could rest on top of him. As for Thunderbird, he was also huge. He could carry a whole lake on his broad back. He was so mighty that if he shifted a single feather, he could unleash thunder and make the lake send a torrent of water cascading to earth.

One day, Thunderbird landed on Whale's back. He dug his sharp talons into Whale's flesh. Desperate to dislodge Thunderbird, Whale dove to the deepest part of the ocean. But though Thunderbird was dragged underwater, he wouldn't let go. As the two struggled and thrashed, their battle unleashed a mighty buckling of the earth and ocean.

The story of Thunderbird and Whale is a memorable way to tell the story of an earthquake and a tsunami.

A Mohawk elder is speaking at a council meeting. In her hand, she holds a story belt, woven with reminders of what she wishes to say.

Storytellers sometimes used stone carvings, shells, rugs, or pottery to illustrate the stories they were telling or to jog their memories. This wampum belt is a reminder for the Haudenosaunee people, who live near the Great Lakes. Special symbols and details of events were woven into wampum belts to act as cues to the storyteller.

THE STORY SCIENCE TELLS

Archaeology is a science that gives us another way to discover the past. Archaeologists study physical remains to piece together what happened thousands, or even millions, of years ago.

We leave traces behind after we are gone: our tools, clothing, art, garbage, and even bones and teeth. Over time, floods or landslides, or layers of earth, rocks, or water can cover those traces. Archaeologists uncover those signs of life. They dig in the ground, dive underwater, and even use satellite technology to find clues to the past. One small piece of bone or stone can be like a book full of information, if you know how to read it.

HOW OLD IS IT? SCIENCE ANSWERS THE QUESTION

Relative Dating

Archaeologists use relative dating to tell the age of an artifact. Let's say you find a porcelain teacup decorated with violets. If you find porcelain saucers nearby that are the same color, are made of the same material, and have similar decorations of violets, relative dating might lead you to assume the cup and saucers are the same age. Often relative dating takes into account layers of findings, assuming that older objects will be found buried below things that are newer. But relative dating has limits. For instance, soil and the objects in it can be moved by flowing water, construction work, and even worms.

In the Northwest, totem poles, often carved from huge red cedar trees, are a way to record and remember important events from the past.

Absolute Dating

Absolute dating methods are much more accurate.

Archaeology students at Nipissing University work on an excavation site on Nipissing First Nation territory.

RADIOCARBON DATING: The tissues of every living thing absorb ordinary carbon and radioactive carbon. At death, the radioactive carbon starts to decay. Because scientists know the rate of decay, they can tell when death occurred.

POTASSIUM ARGON DATING: Rocks and stone can't be dated with radioactive carbon, but scientists know that when rocks are formed they contain tiny amounts of radioactive substance. From the time a rock is created, the radioactive material starts to disappear. Because we know how long that loss takes, we can tell when the rock was formed.

LUMINESCENCE DATING: This method is used to date artifacts such as pottery. If a sample is burned at high heat, it will give off a different color depending on its age. This is an accurate method, but it also means damaging the artifact.

THE STORY YOUR IMAGINATION TELLS

There's one more way to discover the past, and that is by using your own imagination. You can begin to understand what it was like to live in a different time or place only if you imagine yourself there. Your imagination can fill in the gaps between myths and science to help make long-ago people come alive to you: What do you think they cared about? What did they think was funny? What songs did they sing? What hopes and dreams did they have?

Myths, science, and imagination—together, they form a map of Turtle Island.

Arctic Ocean

Beringia

Siberia

Bering
Sea

North
America

Pacific
Ocean

Meadowcro

Japan

Monte Verde

Yucatán

Chapter 2

North America in the Days of Ice

100,000 to 13,000 years ago

THE ICE AGE

★ When—and how—did people first come to North America?

★ Visit the Ice Age: the land, the animals, and the people

ARRIVAL
A Mystery Story

Nobody agrees on exactly when or how the story of human life in North America begins. Archaeological evidence, such as bones and stone tools, tells us that human beings had to cross Asia to get to North America from Africa. We can only guess why. Perhaps they were fleeing enemies, or maybe they were following herds of game animals—or maybe they just wanted to know what lay beyond the next hill or river.

We may never know why people arrived in North America, but we are beginning to learn when and how they came.

DID THEY COME BY LAND?

Think of the very highest mountains you can name: Denali, Everest, Kilimanjaro. Around 110,000 years ago, those mountains were invisible under the thick layer of ice that covered much of the earth. The ice was 3.2 km (2 miles) thick in places, and so forbidding and cold that nothing could live on it. So much water was locked up in the ice that sea levels were far lower

A TIME CAPSULE

The first ancestors of humanity, called *hominins*, lived around 6 million years ago. This seems like a long time, but in terms of the earth's history—about 4 billion years—it is the blink of an eye. Hominins branched into different groups, and around 200,000 years ago one of those branches became our direct ancestors, *Homo sapiens*. We know this from bones and teeth that have been found in Africa. Our ancestors began to spread out from Africa 75,000 years ago, eventually reaching all the other continents.

than they are now. The seas that remained were frigid because they were studded with icebergs that had broken off the ice fields.

As the sea level dropped, a new land we call Beringia appeared, joining Asia and Alaska. It is underwater now, but Beringia was once a huge expanse crisscrossed by rivers and covered in grasslands. Though it is sometimes called a land bridge, Beringia stretched 1,609 km (1,000 miles) from north to south.

Beringia was warm enough to live in for humans and the game they hunted. Generations of hunters followed animals farther and farther east until, without realizing it, they had reached a new continent, at least 14,000 years ago.

Once people got across Beringia to what is now called Alaska, they would have found their way blocked by cold, barren areas that led to immense fields of ice. When the Ice Age was coming to an end around 13,000 years ago, a passage opened up through the ice fields. Animals and the people who hunted them now had a path to follow south, and they kept going, right to the farthest tip of South America.

An artist imagines people walking across Beringia. It took many generations of people gradually moving east as they followed game. Animals and humans must have stayed away from the ice fields because there were no plants and no game to eat there, and there was always the danger of sudden floods.

NEW EVIDENCE SHAKES AN OLD THEORY

The theory that the only way south was by foot through the ice passage has been turned upside down, thanks in part to new research methods that allow archaeologists to uncover signs of human life that are far south of that ice-free corridor, and far apart from each other and from Beringia.

Meadowcroft, Pennsylvania

On November 12, 1955, a farmer named Albert Miller out walking his fields near Pittsburgh, Pennsylvania, found some old bones in a groundhog burrow. His find led to the discovery of what was soon known as Meadowcroft Rockshelter, a site that changed our ideas of how people settled North America. American archaeologist James Adovasio began to dig at the Meadowcroft Rockshelter and eventually unearthed millions of signs left by human beings—bits of bones and stones, charcoal from fire pits, and even scraps of weaving. Radiocarbon dating showed that these artifacts were anywhere from 16,000 to 19,000 years old—in other words, from the Ice Age. The ice fields were swept by endless roaring winds, and from time to time, floods of water gushed out from under the ice, drowning everything in their path. Crossing them would have been an impossible challenge for those first people.

And yet humans were sitting in a rock shelter in Meadowcroft, roasting deer on a spit, when a vast field of ice separated them from Beringia.

Monte Verde, Central Chile

Adding to the mystery, other places where humans once settled have been found. In 1978 American anthropologist Thomas D. Dillehay was digging at an archaeological site in south-central Chile called Monte Verde. He and his colleagues found stone and bone tools, traces of wooden buildings, partially chewed plants, and even a teenager's footstep preserved in clay. Radiocarbon dating revealed the site to be 12,500 years old.

Yucatán, Mexico

In 2008, Mexican cave divers found more new evidence that made scientists question how humans came to the Americas. They were diving in an underwater cave in Yucatán, Mexico, when, to their amazement, they found human bones buried in the cave's floor. The bones were those of a young woman. Hers are the oldest human remains found in North America. Nobody knows her real name, so the divers called her Eva.

The cave was not underwater 13,600 years ago when Eva died. Her people must have taken a lot of trouble to bury her because they carried her body along a dark, twisting, underground passage almost half a kilometer (a quarter of a mile) from the cave's opening to the spot that would be her grave.

Archaeologists named her 'Naia. She was a teenaged girl who lived 12,000 to 13,000 years ago. Her remains were found in a cave in Hoyo Negro, Mexico. Though it was dry when 'Naia lived and died, the cave is now flooded. A diver brushes debris from her skull.

ALL THIS EVIDENCE was a puzzle for scientists. How could people be living as far away and as far apart as Pennsylvania 16,000 years ago, Chile 12,500 years ago, and Mexico 13,600 years ago when in those times the way from Beringia was blocked by ice?

What if Beringia wasn't the only way to North America?

DID THEY COME BY SEA?

The first human beings to reach North America may have followed the northern coastline of the Pacific Ocean from Asia. The North Pacific Current would have aided their travels as they paddled their boats from present-day Japan or Siberia.

On Triquet Island, off the central coast of British Columbia, archaeologists from the University of Victoria discovered a site that was once a village occupied by the ancestors of the Heiltsuk people. Further excavations uncovered evidence that people had lived there since ancient times. Radiocarbon dating showed the artifacts to be over 14,000 years old.

HAIDA GWAII

.... 14,000 YEARS AGO

The ocean is rough. The animal skin sail is taut against the mast. The men and women aboard the small boat strain their arms as they paddle amid the waves. Salty water sprays into the air, and the mist stings their eyes so that they can hardly tell where the sea ends and the sky begins. They have been traveling so long that their legs cramp as they kneel on the bottom of their animal hide boat. One of them makes sure the embers from the last fire stayed lit in the little cedar box. Inside the box, hot coals smolder in a bed of dried moss, and a lid seals the box, keeping the contents dry. At last the people hear the waves clawing at the shore. They feel a bump and a scrape. Wearily, they slog ashore, dragging the boat as far up onto the beach as they can. They are piling up rocks for a shelter when they hear a terrible sound. A rogue wave has picked up their boat and carried it out to sea. There is no turning back. They will have to make this place their home.

ANY TRACES THAT ANCIENT PEOPLE traveling by sea might have left behind are underwater now because the coastline those early seafarers would have traveled was very different. Seawater locked in the ice fields created a coastline many miles farther out than it is today. Advances in underwater diving gear have made it possible for archaeologists to gather data about ancient shorelines and find traces of human life that might otherwise be lost under ocean waters.

In 2014, underwater archaeologists surveying the frigid waters off Haida Gwaii with sonar equipment found signs that what is now the seabed was once dry land dotted with rivers and lakes. The archaeologists made another stunning discovery: under the water they found the remains of stone structures that might have been built 13,700 years ago. If so, they would be the earliest signs of human life in Canada.

Underwater archaeology is a new way to explore the past. An underwater archaeologist works off the shore of Haida Gwaii, far below the ocean's surface.

CAN WE SOLVE THE MYSTERY?

There may be no single answer to the question of how and when the first humans arrived in North America. Some probably came by land across Beringia, while others crossed the Pacific Ocean by boat. We know that they didn't come in a single group with a destination in mind, and they came over thousands of years. When, and in how many waves of new people? We aren't sure.

What's more important than how and when is what life was like for people once they got here.

If you were a time traveler going back to when people first lived in North America, you might think you were visiting a different planet. In many ways, you'd be right.

WHAT WAS THE ENVIRONMENT LIKE?

You might have trouble recognizing the land as the North America that appears on modern maps. If you wanted to find the east coast you'd have to go hundreds of miles farther east to come to it. As for the west coast, it was 81 km (50 miles) farther west than it is today.

The Mississippi River was much smaller, and a glacier was in the process of making a path from the Great Lakes to form the St. Lawrence River. Lands that were once covered in beech, hickory, oak, and blue spruce trees became dry as deserts spread north from the Gulf of California.

UNDERWATER ARCHAEOLOGY

The waters off Haida Gwaii can be as deep as 3 km (1.9 miles). Before diving began, archaeologists from the Canadian National Parks Service ran a test. Sometimes science is supersimple: they dropped a clamshell bucket down 50 m (164 feet) to retrieve soil from the ocean bed. When they pulled up a bucket full of sediment, they found a slate blade. Though the bucket operation was only a preliminary test, the slate blade was evidence that people had probably lived on that long-submerged coast.

WHAT WERE THE ANIMALS LIKE?

The animals you might see if you traveled back to the Ice Age would astonish you. You'd find yourself in the days of megafauna—literally, large animals. You'd see herds of enormous woolly mammoth lumbering through the tall grasses. Camels, on the other hand, were much smaller than their modern descendants. Ancient horses, while smaller than the ones we ride today—about the size of a white-tailed deer—were still recognizable. If you were very quiet, you might come across a lone mastodon crunching twigs and spruce needles at the edge of the forest. And if you ventured into the forest, you might startle a giant sloth as big as a car. You certainly wouldn't want to surprise a short-faced bear, which was taller than a grizzly and faster than a horse.

THE VUNTUT GWITCHIN FIRST NATION

The Gwitchin people occupy a homeland that includes the Yukon, the northwest part of NWT, and parts of Alaska. The Vuntut Gwitchin live in the only Yukon community north of the Arctic Circle. The bluffs and banks along the Old Crow River have been their home since ancient times. The area is the richest source of Ice Age fossils in Canada. Since 1995, their government has owned and managed all the fossils.

Woolly mammoths had tusks that could grow as long as 4.5 meters (15 feet) and had long shaggy coats to help them survive the Ice Age.

Beaver's Transformation

Once Beaver was as large as a black bear—so large that he was able to build a dam across the Yukon River. Ch'ataiiyùukaih, the Traveler, transformed Beaver and the other large animals into smaller ones so that they would not be such a danger to humans.

WHAT WERE THE PEOPLE LIKE?

What way of life equipped people to live in those times of gigantic animals and bone-chilling weather? Using your imagination can help you understand how those long-ago humans saw their world.

In many ways their lives might seem to have been desperately hard and much narrower than ours. They lived in small groups of probably around twenty people. Most of them likely knew only around fifty other individuals, which would be hard for a group trying to survive. People have to find mates so they can have children to replace those who die, which isn't easy if you know so few people. People hunted animals that would provide them with food, shelter, and tools. They would have seen others in their group die, even babies and little children. Their lifespans were shorter than ours today. They were elders if they lived to be thirty, and lucky if they lived to be forty.

In many other ways, ancient people knew a much wider world than ours. There was no such thing as being indoors. Other than rock shelters, they lived all their lives in the open air, with nothing but the horizon limiting their sense of space.

Their country foods were the animals and plants, and if those died out, they would have to find new food sources. They lived in a boundless spiritual world where animals, plants, and humans were equally important because all life is connected.

Despite the differences, in the most important ways those early people were like us. They had the same ability to think, to work out problems, and to use language to communicate. They knew how to work together. They must have had grudges to settle, hurt feelings to soothe, and love stories to tell.

imagine A DAY IN YOUR LIFE

.... 13,600 YEARS AGO

You wake before dawn, when the first birds begin to sing. A quick glance around and you see your family still asleep, wrapped in fur blankets under the shelter of an over-hanging rock. You tie on your woven sandals. With your dog at your heels, you walk the path to the stream to check the fish traps. Once this chore is done, you bring back water in a bag made from a deer's stomach. You check the supply of kindling for the cooking fire.

When the sun comes up, you gather plants. You avoid those that are poisonous and keep a watchful eye out for plants to eat or to use in weaving. All the women and men know how to weave plant fibers into baskets, sandals, and hunting nets. You are proud that you know how to make a net and how to mend it when it gets torn.

When hunting time nears, you help the women and men set out the nets. You will use the nets to snare rabbits today. A successful hunt depends on teamwork. If you don't cooperate and communicate, nobody will have anything to eat. Communication is just as much a part of survival as the food you catch. Your chilly fingers are used to the frustrating work of chipping flakes off stones to make sharp blades for cutting up the game.

Later, while the meat is roasting on a spit over the fire, you work on your sewing. Ever since you've been old enough to handle a delicate bone needle without snapping it in two, you've sewn warm clothes from animal pelts to ward off the biting cold.

Chores take up most of the day, but there is time for fun, too. You and your friends like to make yourselves look nice. Sometimes you make dyes from plants so you can tattoo beautiful patterns onto your friends' skin. You make anklets and necklaces from shells to wear at special ceremonies. You enjoy singing and dancing together.

At the end of the day, you take shelter under the rocky overhang, and curl up side by side with your family. The dogs will bark a warning if any dangerous animals come near, and the fire will glow through the night. Beyond the overhang you can see a sliver of brilliant night sky. You listen to your grandmother tell stories about the stars and the moon until you fall asleep.

The "tool kit" of Ice Age people—the ability to communicate, to make fire, to weave, to sew, to make stone and bone tools, to hunt and to gather plants, and to domesticate dogs—helped them survive for thousands of years.

DOGS: Faithful Companions

Scientists believe dogs probably developed around 30,000 years ago; they've lived side by side with people ever since. As humans spread over the Americas from northeast Asia, dogs came with them. Dogs were the first domestic animals to live with Indigenous people. Although dogs had a close kinship with wolves and coyotes, they were valued as hunters and guards, and they were used to haul trade goods such as furs. Most of all, they were faithful companions.

THE ICE AGE ENDS

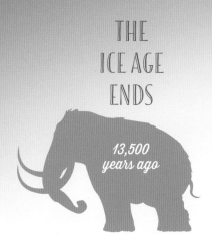

13,500 years ago

When the Ice Age ended, everything changed: the climate, the animals, and the very shape of the land itself. And then, by 11,000 years ago, North America was transformed into a very different place than it had been when the first humans lived here.

Summers became longer and warmer, while winters became shorter. The change in the climate created stress for plant and animal life. Many plants didn't survive. The animals that depended on those plants had less and less to eat. Three-quarters of the animal species that once roamed North America died out. Mammoths and four-horned antelope vanished first. Horses, ground sloths, and camels soon followed. Mastodons held out longer, but eventually they were gone, too. Only the Ice Age bison, which became smaller, still survive.

Though all of this took between 2,000 and 3,000 years to happen, that is a very short time in the world's history. Human beings didn't have much time to learn how to live with different plants and animals. As everything around them changed, they faced an incredible challenge: adapt to the changes—or die out along with the mammoths and mastodons.

Chapter 3

Listening to the Land

8,000 to 3,000 years ago

ADAPTING

★ Meet canoe-builders on the Pacific West Coast

★ Go on a prairie buffalo hunt

★ Watch talented southwestern desert artists

★ Take part in the wild rice harvest
in the northeastern forests

"This we all know: all things are connected. Whatever befalls the earth befalls the sons of the earth. Man did not weave the web of life; he is merely a strand in it. Whatever he does to the web, he does to himself."
—*Chief Seattle, 1854*

IF YOU SET OUT on a trip across the country today, chances are you can find familiar stores, eat in familiar restaurants, and stay in the same hotels as if you'd never left home at all. Not so in the past. The people of early history had to adapt the old Ice Age "tool kit" to where they lived in order to survive.

Adaptation is difficult, and there is no guarantee of success. Human history is littered with examples of failed cultures that could not solve the challenges they faced. Many more groups of people have disappeared than have survived.

Where people did survive, their myths remind us that they saw their lives intertwined with plants, animals, and the very land itself. Those resourceful early humans found ways to live in incredibly different places: on foggy sea-coasts, in rocky canyons, on grassy plains, and at the edge of forests.

WHAT IS ADAPTATION?

Adaptation is the process that helps us find ways to live in different environments. Animals have adaptations, too. A deer has a coat that looks like the forest around it, so its predators have a hard time seeing it. Plants also have adaptations. A cactus and other desert plants can store water, but rain-forest plants often have waxy surfaces so water drips off them. Because humans are so good at adaptation, we can survive in all kinds of environments.

LIFE BY THE OCEAN
The Canoe-Makers of Haida Gwaii

8,000 years ago

The people of Haida Gwaii lived on several islands surrounded by cold Pacific waters. They flourished in their foggy, damp villages thanks in part to the tall cedars that grew along the coast, and to the canoes they crafted from the cedars.

The canoe-makers of Haida Gwaii began by choosing strong cedar logs. Each log would become a single canoe. Some logs were only 1.8 m (6 feet) long and would become canoes for one or two paddlers. Others were a massive 18.3 m (60 feet) long and would become canoes that could carry up to forty people. The canoe-makers spent the autumn hollowing out the logs with stone and bone tools.

Once the snow fell, the canoe-makers were able to slide the roughed-out canoes down to the beach, where they finished them. By the time the spring came the canoes were ready. They would be paddled to the mainland, where some of them would be traded for otter and fox furs and moose and deer meat.

Of course, the people of Haida Gwaii also kept canoes for their own use. They paddled out to sea to fish for salmon and halibut and to hunt whales and seals, enough to feed the people in a hundred villages spread across the islands. The largest canoes were loaded with tons of dried fish and furs to trade as far south as California.

Canoe-making is still an important part of Haida life. A traditional canoe makes a ceremonial trip from Haida Gwaii to Juneau, Alaska.

The Origin of Yellow Cedar

Raven, the great creator and trickster, met three young women drying salmon on the beach. Raven was always hungry, and the salmon looked tempting. He had to get the women away so that he could eat the salmon himself.

"Aren't you afraid of bears?" he asked.

"No," they replied.

"Aren't you afraid of wolves?" he asked.

"No," they replied.

But when he asked, "Aren't you afraid of owls?" they answered, "Yes."

Raven hid himself in some bushes and made owl cries. The terrified women ran up the side of a mountain. There they were turned into cedar trees. To this day, cedars are beautiful: their silky bark and long branches make them look like women.

RAVEN

As in many Indigenous cultures, Raven is a revered hero for the Haida, helping to shape the world for the people. He can also be a trickster. Plenty of stories tell about his pranks. Raven is called by many names in Haida myths, but this doesn't confuse anybody. Like Raven, Haida men may have more than one name.

LIFE ON THE PRAIRIES
The Hunters of Head-Smashed-In Buffalo Jump

6,000 years ago

Far from sea-bound Haida Gwaii, east of the Rocky Mountains, grasslands spread for thousands of miles. The people who lived on the grassy plains knew the ways of the buffalo and felt a strong spiritual connection with them. No wonder, because the buffalo gave people the necessities of life: food, shelter, and clothing.

Hunting buffalo in those early years before anybody had a horse to ride or a bow and arrow to hunt with, much less a rifle, took great stealth and a lot of bravery. The animals were smaller than the ones we see today, but they still weighed more than a ton.

Once the killing was over, the buffalo hides were removed. The animals were cut into pieces, and the choice bits of meat were divided up. Nobody could eat all the meat of dozens of animals killed at the same time, so most of it was dried into pemmican. The long bones were broken so people could eat the marrow. Bones were turned into clubs, knives, and digging tools. The hides were used to make moccasins, drums, cradles, and toy dolls. The horns made good cups and fire carriers. The sinews were used as thread to sew clothes and shelters, the tail for brushes, and the chips for fuel. So that other creatures could also benefit from the buffalo bounty, once the people had taken their share, they left behind a good amount of meat and bones for the Plains grizzly bears, wolves, wolverines, coyotes, vultures, and other birds.

Nervously, you put on your animal hide and hope it will fool the buffalo. Your job is to find the animals and lure them to the cliffs.

Almost everybody in the settlement is at the ceremony to show thanks to the animals about to be killed and to ask that everyone will return safely. The shaman calls with his eagle-bone whistle and waves a tiny spearhead, harnessing its powers to help the hunters. The hunters form V-shaped drive lanes that will channel the herds to the most dangerous part of the cliffs. Near the cliff area of the drive lanes, you and the other buffalo runners hide behind bushes and rocks. You shout at the animals to keep any from wandering away from the herd. When the animals get near the cliff edge, you rush out, panicking the buffalo into a thundering, headlong plunge to their deaths.

More hunters wait below. They kill every animal, even those that are only injured. If any buffalo survive, they could warn the rest. That would be a disaster; nobody could survive without the buffalo.

Hunters round up buffalo using a "surround." The hunters in this painting from 1853 ride horses, an advantage their ancestors didn't have. For thousands of years before, people on the Plains conducted buffalo hunts on foot.

The Story of Weasel Woman

The wolves showed the people how to live by hunting, but still, life was hard, and people knew hunger. No matter how they tried, no buffalo would go into their traps.

Weasel Woman was collecting water from a river near her camp when she saw a herd of buffalo in the distance. She said aloud that she would marry the chief of the buffalo if he would send some of his children into their traps. When she next went to the river, she heard someone calling from the bushes. She turned around to see a young man. He introduced himself as the chief of the buffalo. He said he had heard her call to him. He gave her some small stone buffalo and explained how to use them in a ceremony that would call the buffalo toward a buffalo jump.

Weasel Woman took the buffalo-calling stones back to the camp. She told the spiritual leaders about the ceremony to call the buffalo. They performed the ceremony, and soon they had meat for their meals and more. Ever after, Blackfoot hunters used the buffalo stones to ensure a successful hunt. When Weasel Woman went down to the river again, she met the chief of the buffalo, who transformed her into a buffalo so she could join the herd as his wife.

PEMMICAN: A Superfood

Pemmican can be made from beef, venison, caribou, moose, buffalo, or salmon. After the meat is dried it is pounded up with an equal amount of melted animal fat. Dried fruit can be added: saskatoon berries, cranberries, cherries, and blueberries all make the pemmican delicious, and they add nutrients such as vitamin C.

Nutritious, portable pemmican can last for months or even years. It is an excellent staple that tides people over when other food is scarce.

LIFE IN THE DESERT
The Sacred Art of the Lower Pecos

4,000 years ago

Once herds of camels, horses, and buffalo roamed the Lower Pecos, the remote southwest corner of what is now called Texas. When the climate got warmer, several plants disappeared, and the animals that fed on those plants disappeared, too. The people who settled there could no longer rely on the buffalo, as did those who lived on the Plains. They had to find a different way to live.

The Lower Pecos was blisteringly hot, unpredictable, and dangerous. A misstep could mean a poisonous snake or spider bite. A gentle rainfall could suddenly give way to a raging flash flood. Yet people managed to survive there. Despite the hardships they endured, they sustained themselves with imagination and art.

In our modern world we don't think of art as being important to our survival. Yet the desire to make art is as old as human life on earth. Making art helps us figure out our world and our place in it. From the most ancient times, our ancestors have known that art is a necessity of life.

The most complex and intricate prehistoric rock art in the world is in the Lower Pecos. For centuries, artists used the walls of rock shelters to create an amazing array of petroglyphs (images "pecked" slowly and painstakingly into the rock face with stone tools) and pictographs (images painted with ground-up charcoal, ocher, or minerals such as manganese, which can provide black or brown pigment). On the surface of the rocks you can still see where the paint was ground.

The sheer number of pieces of art in the rock shelters of the Lower Pecos is staggering—there are thousands of multicolored deer, wild cats, dogs, and wolves, and geometric patterns such as lightning bolts and arches that seem to show that the real world is separate from the spirit world above.

WERE THE IMAGES MEANT to communicate with spirits to make the people successful in the hunt, or to thank the animals for their lives? Were they meant to heal wounded bodies or souls who were in despair? Or were they the record of an artist's dream or trance? The art looks like it tells stories, but the stories themselves are lost to us. We only know that they show magical flights, animals and humans transforming into one another, and that there's another world besides the one we live in. This was sacred work, as vital as food and water to those who made it and understood it.

Families lived under rock overhangs where they were protected from the weather. In this picture from Seminole Canyon State Park in Texas, a mother is grinding grain, against a backdrop of the art that covers the rock face.

You feel a sense of wonder as you enter the yawning mouth of the cave. You have been chosen to be one of those who will hold a torch so the artist can see as she paints.

Every sound you make echoes against the stone walls. Water trickles from the roof. Now and then a cool drop of it hits your torch and makes it sizzle.

The artist runs her hand across the face of the rock, carefully tracing every crack and bulge. She will include them in her picture. There are already paintings of deer, mountain lions, fish, and birds another artist once painted. They, too, will become part of her painting, connecting her with her ancestors and the animals.

You hold the torch steady as she works. A figure—part human, part animal—with feathers, wings, and antlers seems to emerge from the rock itself. The figure holds plants and darts, sticks and pouches in its hand. The plants, darts, sticks, and pouches are all signs of a shaman, who can contact guardian spirits while in a trance, and this art is a record of the shaman's power.

You try to remember every detail because what you are witnessing is sacred.

As you are about to leave the cave, the artist nods at you. A feeling of awe washes through you as you dip your hand into the dye and press it to the rock face.

THE SUN-FATHER

Art was so important that it was part of the creation myth of the Zuni people, whose stories say they are the descendants of painters. The stories describe the people of early times as being as dark as their cave homes, with cold, scaly skin, eyes as round as an owl's, and ears as pointed as a bat's. They had webbed feet and they had tails. They crouched when they walked, like they did in the caves. When they left their caves they cried out at the brightness. The Sun-Father heated them by his light and glory.

RECIPE
Turn a Poisonous Plant into Dinner

The people of the Lower Pecos had to be inventive when it came to finding food. The lechuguilla plant looks like a fistful of green fingers fringed with thorns. Its leaves could be woven into sandals tough enough to protect feet against the scorching ground. The fibers made sturdy sleeping mats and baskets. The plant could even be turned into a good shampoo, as long as you were careful not to get any in your mouth—the sap was so poisonous it could kill a rabbit. Yet people found a way to turn this plant into delicious food using the first ovens ever found in North America.

Prickly, tough lechuguilla plants grow in the hot Chihuahuan Desert in Big Bend National Park, Texas.

Someone had to collect wood, which was scarce in the desert. The wood was allowed to burn down to hot coals and rocks. Then cactus pads were piled on top. The pads, full of water, let off steam as they got hot. The lechuguilla was baked for two days, neutralizing the poison. Then it was pounded into patties that would keep for months. The poisonous, spiky plant had been turned into a sweet and healthy food that was well worth the work.

Artists carved images of long-horn sheep, deer, what may be a bat, and a hunter with a bow and arrow into sandstone.

LIFE BY THE GREAT LAKES
The Wild Rice Reapers of Paradise Point

4,000 years ago

The woodlands around the Great Lakes were much more hospitable than the Lower Pecos. Here, one of the challenges was to live in harmony with the four seasons, to take advantage of times when plants and game were plentiful, and to prepare for harsh, snowy times when food was scarce.

Two or three families often lived in a small settlement to wait out the winter. They had to find a way to survive when snow blanketed everything and game animals were hibernating. By gathering wild rice in the summer they were able to stave off starvation through the lonely and hungry months of winter.

For two or three weeks at the end of summer, dozens of family groups gathered at what is now called Paradise Point in Hamilton, Ontario, for the wild rice harvest. This harvest must have been a joyous time when friends who hadn't seen one another in a year could get together. Adults were sure to make comments about how much the children had grown. The older people were likely to tease the younger ones about who would be ready to marry soon. Tears would be shed for those who had died since everyone had last been together.

Traditions that are still practiced where wild rice is grown let us imagine how the rice must have been harvested at Paradise Point.

A man poled a canoe out into the marsh. Two of the women in the family sat in the canoe and each used a stick to bend the rice stalks—which can grow to 2.1 m (7 feet)—to knock the kernels into the bottom of the canoe. Back on land, the kernels were spread out on mats to dry in the sun. Once it is dry, wild rice will last for ages, making it a good crop to have at home when the snow covers everything and the animals are hibernating.

A family works together to knock kernels of wild rice into the bottom of their canoe.

How Wild Rice Was Given to the People

The Anishinaabe people once lived along the Atlantic coast. Spirits directed them to travel west until they came to a place where they would find "food that grows on water." When they got to the Great Lakes, they saw broad beds of wild rice.

The hero Nanaboozhoo learned about rice from a duck. One evening he came home from hunting without any game for his supper. A duck was perched on the edge of his kettle of boiling water. The duck flew off at Nanaboozhoo's approach. Nanaboozhoo peered into the kettle. Wild rice, or manoomin, was floating on the water. He had never tasted anything better. He followed the duck until he came to a lake full of manoomin. This was surely a gift from the Creator.

THE PEOPLE OF HAIDA GWAII, Head-Smashed-In Buffalo Jump, the Lower Pecos, and Paradise Point lived in very different places. By paying attention to the land and living in harmony with it, they were able to adapt to and make the best of living by the sea, on the prairies, on the desert, or in the woodlands.

Years passed. Change happened, but it happened slowly. If you were born during those centuries, you could expect to live much like your parents had.

Ojibwa artist Daphne Odjig wanted to make sure that Ojibwa children knew about their cultural heroes. She created several books featuring Nanabush as a young boy children could relate to. This painting is called *Nanabush and the Beavers*.

NANABOOZHOO

Nanaboozhoo (or Nanabush) is an important culture character for the Anishinaabe. Nanaboozhoo is a shape-shifter who teaches right from wrong through all his adventures. He teaches the people how to live in harmony with nature.

Mexico

Pacific
Ocean

San José
Mogote

San
Lorenzo

To protect their corn, farmers
bang on pots to scare the birds
away from their crop.

Chapter 4

Ideas Spread

3,000 years ago

NEW IDEAS

★ Giant heads, rubber balls, corn:
How did they change life across North America?

WE HUMANS KNOW GOOD IDEAS when we see them. New ideas that today can be shared with the click of a button used to be carried by invaders, by enslaved people taken from their homes, by explorers, but most often by traders. The people of Turtle Island were skillful traders. Thanks to them, the trade routes that crisscrossed the continent became highways for ideas.

You had to have a lot of knowledge to be a trader. You had no printed maps, so you had to know how to read the stars above and the way that rivers flowed. Along the way, you would have to communicate with people who spoke different languages, so you would have to be fluent in sign language. You would have to know the rules of how to behave in a stranger's home. And you'd need amazing stamina to travel hundreds of miles on foot or by canoe, carrying baskets full of goods. You had to keep precious cargo, such as turquoise jewelry or fragile pottery, safe.

☼

EVERY NOW AND THEN an idea comes along that changes everything. We're living in such a time. You probably know people who remember life before computers. When new ideas came from Mexico and Mesoamerica (*meso* means "middle," so Mesoamerica means the land between North and South America), they had the same kind of impact as computers. No borders existed to stop the flow of ideas, and ideas did flow from coast to coast and between north and south.

IDEAS SPREAD
Art and Design

3,600 years ago

The people of North America had a desire for beautiful art and design. They treasured luxury items: jeweled anklets, lavish turbans, fine furs, feathered cloaks, pendants made of mirrors so precisely ground that they could start fires. People fancied they were holding bits of sky in their hands when they held turquoise. The trade routes that linked north and south influenced tastes in art and design across the miles.

You are visiting San Lorenzo, the first city in the Americas. It was built by the Olmec people in what is now Mexico. Everywhere you look you are surrounded by art. The same chunky figures crop up on walls, pottery, tiles, and jewelry. Some figures look like people suffering from leprosy, others like unborn babies. Still others look part jaguar and part human.

The Olmec may appear strange to you, but they have their own ideas of beauty. The nobles tie small, flat pieces of wood to their babies' foreheads to flatten them and make their skulls look longer. The really rich carve deep grooves into their teeth. Jade nose rings are also popular.

Nothing astonishes you as much as the giant stone heads and thrones that stand on the central platform in the city. Each one is taller than a grown man, and you know each can weigh 18 t (20 tons). There are ferocious faces, proud and haughty faces, and faces that look about to burst out laughing. No matter where you go in San Lorenzo, you feel the eyes of a stone king watching your every step.

Wheels weren't used for transportation, so moving anything heavy meant using rafts, organization, and the muscle power of hundreds of people.

Giant Heads

The giant heads of San Lorenzo are the result of mind-boggling effort. First, sculptors chose huge boulders that were roughly shaped like human heads. Olmec artists knew how to make wheels, but they used them only for toys and ceremonial objects, so humans must have rolled these enormous boulders of basalt on logs for up to 150 km (93 miles) to bring them to San Lorenzo.

Next, sculptors used hammer stones, made of the same basalt as the boulders, to chip away the features. Finally, abrasives were used to finish the sculptures. The backs of most of the heads were left flat. They were probably recarved, perhaps when a new king came to the throne and wanted his image preserved in rock.

When archaeologists looked at the giant heads in the context of where they were found, they discovered that other sculptures had been stored or recarved around them. That means the heads weren't untouchable idols in sacred places. They were probably grouped together to act out events from myths or history. The effort that went into the giant heads was worthy of a king. After all, the kings were the go-betweens between the spiritual life of the heavens, the physical life on the earth, and the underworld.

Around 2,400 years ago, either a revolution or an invasion toppled the nobles of San Lorenzo, and the stone heads along with them. But the styles in the art, jewelry, and sculpture of San Lorenzo influenced tastes in North America.

This colossal Olmec carved head from Vera Cruz, Mexico, is 5.2 m (17 feet). It probably represents a king. Ball games were so important that he is shown wearing a helmet, like the one he would have worn when playing an Olmec ball game.

An archaeologist is careful not to disturb or harm what she has found. In this case, it's an ammonite fossil, left by a shelled creature that lived more than 65 million years ago.

AN ARCHAEOLOGIST'S TOOL: "Context"

To understand the Olmec giant heads, archaeologists used an idea called context. Examining context is like detective work, finding associations with other objects, architecture, and people to help us interpret information about an artifact.

Suppose you find an arrowhead. Carefully, you brush away the soil around it. Next, you record exactly where you found it. Now comes the hard work:

- Are there other arrowheads near it? If there are, was this a place where a toolmaker used to work? Or did a battle once rage here? If no other arrowheads are around, did this one belong to a lone hunter who left home to stalk his prey?
- Have similar arrowheads been found in other places? If so, do they tell us the size of the territory where the person or people once hunted?
- What is the arrowhead made of? If it is made of bone, metal, or stone from far away, did somebody trade for it or travel far to get it?
- What else is around the arrowhead? Is it embedded in the skeleton of a mastodon, or does it rest beside the bones of somebody who treasured it so much that he wanted it near him for eternity?
- How old is it? Did you find it under a now-extinct animal or on top of a modern horse skeleton?

Fluted projectile points were used 13,500 years ago. They are called Clovis Points because they were first found in Clovis, New Mexico, in 1929.

IDEAS SPREAD
Play Ball!

3,800 years ago

A modern-day Mayan ballplayer takes part in an ancient Mayan ball game in a park in Guatemala City.

Slash the bark of the rubber tree (*Castilla elastica*), and use a cup to collect the latex—the sticky, raw liquid that runs from it. Then take the vine from a kind of morning glory, strip off the leaves and flowers, and wrap the vine into a coil. Next, beat it on a rock so you can squeeze out its juice. Mix the morning glory juice with the latex, and stir it. It will turn into a white mass. The result? Rubber.

Once the Olmec chemists figured out how to make rubber, they found dozens of ways to use it. They shaped it into figures of humans and animals. They made rubber bands to hold the heads of axes to their wooden handles. Rubber was turned into paint and medicine. Most important, rubber was formed into bouncy balls. And that led to ball games.

Olmec ball games were violent and dangerous. Players wore leather helmets, knee and arm pads, chest protectors, gloves, and "yokes" to protect their hips. No wonder—the balls used for hip ball may have weighed up to 4 kg (9 pounds)! Ball games were such a big part of life that the giant heads of San Lorenzo wear carved ball game helmets.

Rubber balls were used for games that were part religious ritual, part action sport, and part politics. Typically, athletic men played these games, and perhaps women, too, but everyone was involved, whether in playing, cheering, or betting on the outcome.

In one game, a player had to get the ball through a vertical hoop (not a horizontal one like in basketball). In another game that sounds familiar, players hit the ball with a stick or bat. The most popular was the "hip game," whose aim was to put the ball into the opponent's end zone using only your hips—no hands or feet.

Ball games quickly spread and became an exciting part of life for people all over North America, whether or not they were played with rubber balls.

IDEAS SPREAD
Corn Comes to North America

2,500 years ago

If you like french fries, pizza, or chocolate, you can thank the people of the Western Hemisphere (modern-day South America, Central America, and North America). They discovered that potatoes, tomatoes, chocolate, peanuts, beans, squash, Jerusalem artichokes, sweet potatoes, sunflowers, peppers, pineapples, watermelons, cassava, bananas, strawberries, and pecans—in fact, at least half the foods we think of as staples—are all good to eat.

Of all the ideas shared between south and north, the most important by far was how to grow corn. It would become a way of life for millions of people. If you look at the ingredients in the food on a supermarket shelf, you will see that corn in many forms is still a big part of our diet.

In 1851 Cornelius Krieghoff painted *Indian Family in the Forest*. In his artwork he tried to show his view of what North America's people and scenery were like.

Olmec farmers were growing corn over 6,000 years ago, and by 2,500 years ago people in North America were growing it, too.

Most corn was dried and ground on a thick slab of stone that was roughened to hold the kernels in place. This was efficient, but it also meant that bits of grit got into the meal. Wherever people relied on corn diets, their teeth would be worn down to sore stubs by the time they were adults. Nevertheless, corn quickly became a necessity of life. It was incredibly versatile: ground corn was turned into dumplings and bread, used as a thickener to make hearty stews, and even dropped into water to make a nourishing drink. When it was eaten with squash and beans, it made a balanced diet.

Eventually, corn was grown across North America from the St. Lawrence River to Argentina and Chile in South America. Everywhere it was grown, it was celebrated as a great gift. In the Southwest, the Pueblos cleaned their storage bins before the harvest to make the corn comfortable. On the Plains, people "sang up" their corn through special rituals. The Pawnees grew ten different kinds, including one that was meant only for religious purposes, not for eating. To mark the birth of a Zuni baby, the newborn was given an ear of corn. To the Navajo, corn was sacred because it gave life itself.

"INVENTING" CORN: 7,000 Years Ago

There was no such thing as a wild corn harvest because corn never grew wild. There are fierce arguments among scientists about what plants went into making what we know as corn 7,000 years ago, but they do agree that human beings invented it by observing, experimenting, and getting lucky as they crossbred different plants. Over time, corn has taken all kinds of forms. It can have puny cobs the size of your baby finger with kernels no bigger than an ant, or it can have huge cobs that are 0.6 m (2 feet) long, with each kernel as big and puffy as a piece of popcorn.

Creation in The Book of the People
(The Popul Vuh, written between 1554 and 1558)

The Creator gods first made the earth, then the plants, and then the animals. When it came time to make human beings, the Creator gods first tried mud. But the mud just turned back into mud. Then they tried wood, but wooden creatures don't have minds. Next they tried flesh, but flesh made humans too wicked. At last they tried dough made from corn. It worked. Ever since, human beings were said to consist of corn.

The Popul Vuh *was written in K'iche', a Mayan language, by one or more Mayan authors. It tells how humans were created and what the gods did, and gives a chronology of Mayan kings up to the year 1500.*

IDEAS SPREAD
Writing in
San José Mogote, Mexico

3,000 years ago

If you were to enter one of the temples in San José Mogote, Mexico, 3,000 years ago, you would have had to step on the flat stone that serves as a stoop. Someone carved an image of a grimacing man into that stone. No wonder he's grimacing: his innards bubble out of his side, and drops of blood carved in the stone surround him. The artist who carved the stoop wanted to be sure you knew that this was a crushed enemy, one who would be crushed again and again by the feet of each person who entered the temple. He was sentenced to eternal humiliation.

Between the grimacing man's feet are two lines. They may be his name: "Earthquake." The word *earthquake* is the earliest evidence of writing found in the Americas.

Spaniards slaughter Mochtezuma's followers in this illustration from the *History of the Indies of New Spain*, written in 1581 by Diego Duran. The book is known as the Codex Duran, and is one of the first books by a European about Turtle Island.

CHEROKEE PHOENIX.

NEW ECHOTA, THURSDAY FEBRUARY 21, 1828.

For centuries, until the Spanish arrived in February 1519, the people of Mesoamerica wrote thousands and thousands of books. Priest-scribes wrote science books, biographies of great people, instruction manuals for how to perform rituals, and collections of songs and verses. They recorded the taxes collected for fine cloth, military uniforms, feathered headdresses, disks of gold, exotic plants, and bundles of blankets. They kept detailed family histories—one book listed twenty-six generations of rulers. The texts were painted on paper pounded from the bark of trees that grew in the jungle, folded to look something like present-day comic strips, or folded and stacked like an accordion.

The fate of these books is one of the great tragedies of human history. The Spanish invaders burned whole libraries down. This poem, originally written in a Nahuatl language in 1528, describes the tragedy:

Broken spears lie in the roads;
We have torn out our hair in grief.
The houses are roofless now and their walls
Are red with blood.

THE WRITTEN WORD

Though recording events by writing them down did not become a tradition for most people north of Mexico before 1491, writing has a long history. Between 1826 and 1924, Indigenous communities founded at least fifty newspapers. In 1828, a Cherokee doctor and historian named Emmett Starr started the *Cherokee Phoenix*, a weekly newspaper in the Cherokee language. The Mi'kmaq in Atlantic Canada, the Aleut in Alaska, and the Yaqui in the Southwest, among others, invented writing systems to communicate in and preserve their languages.

Cahokia

Snaketown

Chaco Canyon

Pacific
Ocean

Chapter 5

Change-Makers

2,500 to 1,300 years ago

MEET THE INNOVATORS

★ Dig canals that make the desert bloom in Snaketown

★ Harness solar power in Pueblo Bonito

★ Build mountains in Cahokia

IF YOU COULD GO BACK in time around a thousand years, you would certainly meet seasoned traders of furs, foods, jewelry, and pottery. You'd also meet skilled architects, engineers, and all kinds of craftspeople. In early times, natural forces such as the weather, rivers, mountains, and valleys shaped the conditions for life in North America. Now, across the continent, experts used their knowledge to be the shapers themselves. You could see their work in many places in North America: the extraordinary canal system of the Hohokam that made a garden out of the desert, the first apartment buildings of the Anasazi, and the great city of the Mississippian are just three examples.

THE CANALS OF THE HOHOKAM

2,500 years ago

The Hohokam people settled in the scorching hot valleys around the Salt River, about 40 km (25 miles) south of the modern city of Phoenix, Arizona. They were able to flourish in the desert because they built one of the oldest and best canal systems in the world.

Using pieces of broken pottery and digging sticks, women, men, and children all toiled under the hot sun to dig the broad, shallow canals to bring water from upriver. The water that flowed through the canals irrigated the cotton, beans, squash, and corn planted in small earth mounds. Thanks to their canals, over time the Hohokam turned 28,328 ha (70,000 acres) of desert into fertile vegetable gardens.

Farmers are channeling water that comes from a faraway river to irrigate their crops.

They were able to grow so much food and cotton that they had more than they needed. They used the rest for trade.

The Hohokam had great taste in jewelry. Their traders walked 482 km (300 miles) in the heat to the Pacific coast, carrying bundles of cotton ponchos, belts, and shirts to trade for lustrous shells to string into bracelets, necklaces, and anklets.

imagine YOU ARE AN ARTISAN IN SNAKETOWN

You live in a town that's now called Snaketown in Arizona. It's called Snaketown not because there are plenty of snakes—there are—but because of the serpent designs that decorate pottery and jewelry.

You make your way through the bustling, prosperous settlement, taking a moment to watch athletes practicing maneuvers for a ball game on one of the ball courts. You pass the workshops of potters and weavers. After you exchange greetings, you settle down to make jewelry.

Your family has brought shells back from the coast. You decide that today you won't etch lizards or birds. You will carve a snake into a single piece of clamshell from the Gulf of California. You may decide to keep it for yourself, because when you wear it, everybody will know your clan.

When the day is over, you walk home to the sounds of playing children, barking dogs, and squawking birds. Everybody loves jewel-colored feathers to wear, so they keep their own macaws and parrots. When night falls, the birds finally go to sleep. And so do you, as you listen to the wind and the yip of the coyotes in the cold, clear desert air.

OVER THE YEARS, the Hohokam farmers built more and more complex canals. Smaller ones connected with the larger ones like the threads of a spider's web. Engineers noticed that if the canals were made narrower and deeper, less water was lost by evaporation, so they improved the design. If one of the canals leaked, everybody worked side by side to repair it.

Around a thousand years ago, the thriving Hohokam settlements were abandoned. Why? There are no signs of a single catastrophic flood, disease, or war, but as more people moved to the area, drawn by the farmlands created by the canal waters, the Hohokam faced some very modern problems.

More people means pollution: getting rid of human waste is more difficult, so there is more disease. More abundant crops but fewer varieties of crops were grown, so a bad harvest meant a hungry year. Bit by bit, the population began to decline. Nobody would have noticed a gradual population drop of only 1 or 2 percent each year. Still, small changes add up. By the 1400s about 75 percent of the population was gone. The canal-makers' way of life had lasted for a thousand years. That's longer than almost any other civilization on earth.

HOW DO ARCHAEOLOGISTS ESTIMATE POPULATION?

Archaeologists think that hundreds of people lived in Snaketown at any one time. Their estimate comes from a count of the number of buildings they have found and the number of rooms in each building. Based on those figures, they calculated how many people used each room at one time, and over time. Suppose your family of four lives in a house with three bedrooms. An archaeologist in the distant future would want to know how many different groups of four lived in the house because your three-bedroom house could be home to dozens of people over a century.

APARTMENT LIVING ON THE COLORADO PLATEAU

1,100 to 850 years ago

Across the mountains from the Hohokam, the Anasazi lived in a sun-baked land of flat-topped mesas and rocks the wind carved into eerie shapes. Surviving in that harsh landscape wasn't easy. The Anasazi not only survived there, but also over a period of 300 years, their architects designed some of the most spectacular architecture in North America.

The image of Kokopelli hunched over his flute has been found in art, on pottery, and on jewelry all over Utah, Colorado, Arizona, and New Mexico, but his origin is a mystery. Sometimes he is called a warrior or a roving magician or a trader come north from Mexico. Whether he is a symbol of trade or of the gifts of rain and fertility, he brings happiness with him.

The music the mythical Kokopelli makes on his nose flute chases away the winter and invites the spring to come. The snow melts, and the grass grows green and lush. Once his music has soothed the earth, it is ready to receive seeds that he carries in his hump or in a sack on his back. The seeds will grow and feed the people for another season. Women will get pregnant, and babies will be born.

The Anasazi built the first apartment houses anywhere. The biggest house was the jaw-dropping Pueblo Bonito in Chaco Canyon. Pueblo Bonito, with its high, straight sandstone walls; its graceful design; and its spacious plazas was the work of brilliant engineers and highly skilled craftspeople who made buildings that could house thousands of people at a time.

Not only was Pueblo Bonito beautiful (its name means "beautiful city" in Spanish), but it was also a marvel of smart solar architecture. The walls were positioned to catch the sun's rays, keeping the sandstone warm in the winter but shady in the summer, so the building was as cool as possible despite the brutal heat.

Chaco Canyon grew prosperous because of turquoise. Raw stones were ground into beads and then sold south to Mexico, where they were made into spectacular jewelry. The Tulan people in Mexico were the biggest market for Chaco Canyon turquoise. When the Tulan went to war, they stopped thinking about turquoise, and the economy of Chaco Canyon began to crumble. Then, around 1100, a great drought hit the area. After fifty years of terrible times, the people moved away. Chaco Canyon was abandoned. The remains of Pueblo Bonito still stand in Chaco Canyon.

A silver and turquoise Kokopelli pendant follows a very old tradition. Turquoise jewelry has always been highly prized, and was considered more valuable than gold.

ANASAZI ROAD-BUILDERS

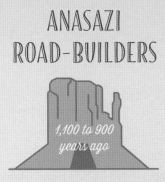

1,100 to 900 years ago

The Anasazi built miles and miles of long, straight roads. The people didn't use wheeled carts or yoked draught animals that would need good roads. Besides, many of the roads didn't seem to lead anywhere. Yet enormous effort was needed to build them and keep them repaired. Why would anybody bother?

The roads weren't built for "practical" reasons at all. They served a far more important purpose: they were built for pilgrims—religious travelers. The Anasazi had a complex way of looking at the universe, the cosmos, with meaning attached to the four directions as well as to the sun, stars, moon, and planets. For them, specific places had a strong spiritual force. The roads they built connected such places. To the people who built the roads and the people who walked them, their meaning was clear and very powerful.

imagine YOU ARE A TRADER TRAVELING TO CAHOKIA ☀

.... 1,500 YEARS AGO

You are on your first trade trip south down the Mississippi River. Your canoe is loaded with furs. The first thing you see is a smudge of smoke in the sky. Soon you can smell hundreds of cooking fires. You can hear the bustle of Cahokia before you see the city. You are used to everyday sounds: the wind rustling leaves and grass, the thick flocks of birds overhead, the buzz of insects, the crash of thunder and lightning. But the kind of noise made by so many people all in one place is something you've never experienced.

When you finally see Cahokia, all you can do is gasp. So much activity! Women are bent double under huge baskets of fish. Others sit by the riverbank mending fishing nets. Tattooed and painted men offer leather pouches of water to a group unloading bundles of copper. You try not to stare at a long canoe as it pushes away from the shore carrying a dozen silent soldiers and their weapons.

Towering over the houses and the busy port of Cahokia is a small mountain. It is the tallest structure you've ever seen.

THE GREAT CITY OF CAHOKIA

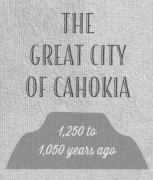

1,250 to 1,050 years ago

People lived next to the Mississippi River and harvested the valley's bountiful country foods such as game, fish, and plants for thousands of years. Starting perhaps as early as 5,000 years ago, they built mounds in an area from present-day Mississippi to Illinois and Idaho, from Ohio west into the Plains. Ten thousand mounds stand in Ohio alone.

There were mounds where sacred ceremonies took place, mounds that were shaped like animals, and mounds that were used for burials. Some mounds served all three purposes. Mounds came in all shapes and sizes: squares, circles, octagons, rectangles, and pyramids. Even the smallest Mississippian hamlets where most people lived usually had a central mound, and each was a feat of planning and effort. Workers moved tons of earth to build them. The largest mound by far was built about 1,250 years ago in a spectacular city along the Mississippi River called Cahokia.

Cahokia was the biggest city anywhere north of Mexico. It was crowded with mounds, dwellings, and dozens of grand plazas for games and ceremonies. Miles of stockades circled Cahokia to ward off enemies. We don't know how many people actually lived in the city at one time. As many as 500 people lived in the center of the city, and no fewer than 4,000 or 5,000 more lived in single-family houses on the floodplain around them. That may not sound like much of a city, but at the time it was built Cahokia was as big as London, England.

Monks Mound sat at the heart of the city. It was an enormous clay platform 30 m (100 feet) tall, roughly 300 m (1,000 feet) long, and 244 m (800 feet) wide at the base. Its four terraces covered 6.5 hectares (16 acres). Monks Mound was the largest single earthwork ever built by the Indigenous people of North America. This one mound meant that more than a mind-boggling 1.9 million m^2 (21 million square feet) of earth had to be shoveled into baskets and carried there.

What inspired people to lug 23-kg (50-pound) bags or baskets of dirt day after day—at least 15 million loads in total—for what must have been years just to build a colossal pile of earth?

People were willing to labor so hard because the mounds had great spiritual importance to them. Mounds, big and small, were sacred places.

The chief lived on the highest point. From there, he could rule his people and speak to the spirits who dwell in the sky. The chief was responsible for maintaining the balance between the upper world and the living world. By serving him, every worker was serving the gods.

An artist imagines the hustle and bustle of a day in Cahokia. Jewelry, pottery, and other goods from all over the continent were bought and sold by traders who traveled great distances with their wares.

DEATH, CAHOKIA STYLE

For centuries people had made mounds to cover the dead, but burials had never been as full of pomp as those at Cahokia. There is evidence of ritual in every pile of earth. In one, two city fathers were buried back to back. One was laid facedown, the other faceup on top of him. Between the two bodies, 20,000 shells from the Gulf of Mexico were arranged in the shape of a falcon.

Around the same time, a second mound was built nearby for the bodies of several other important people. Then, some fifty years later, a third burial mound was built between the first two. More than fifty young women were buried there together. Buried on top of them were four males, their heads and hands removed and their arms wrapped around one another.

A different kind of burial took place near these three mounds around 900 years ago. Thirty-nine men and women stood on the edge of a pit. Each had been clubbed on the back of the head. Three of them were decapitated. They were all buried in the pit—some of them while they were still alive. The bodies were covered by a mat, and fifteen more bodies, most likely those of nobles, were piled on top. Nobody knows if these people offered themselves as sacrifice or were executed.

When Cahokia flourished, it was the largest city north of Mexico. Monks Mound, shown in the background, was the biggest earthwork built in North America.

The Great Serpent Mound in Adams County, Ohio, is nearly half a kilometer (a quarter of a mile) long. It is called an effigy mound because it represents a figure. The serpent's tail is tightly curled into a spiral, while its body slithers over the landscape like a real snake. Its open jaws look like they're holding a giant egg. The egg is actually a burial mound. The people who built the Great Serpent Mound around 2,800 years ago are known by the name Adena.

The Great Serpent Mound follows the serpent's triple-coiled and writhing body to where it ends in an open-mouthed head.

THE MISSISSIPPIAN MOUND-BUILDING way of life lasted for 900 years, making it one of the longest-surviving cultures in history, but Cahokia flourished for no more than 150 years. There is no evidence that there was a war, no traces of earthquake or fire. Nobody knows why Cahokia became a ghost town, though its location on the floodplain of the Mississippi River made it vulnerable to catastrophic flooding.

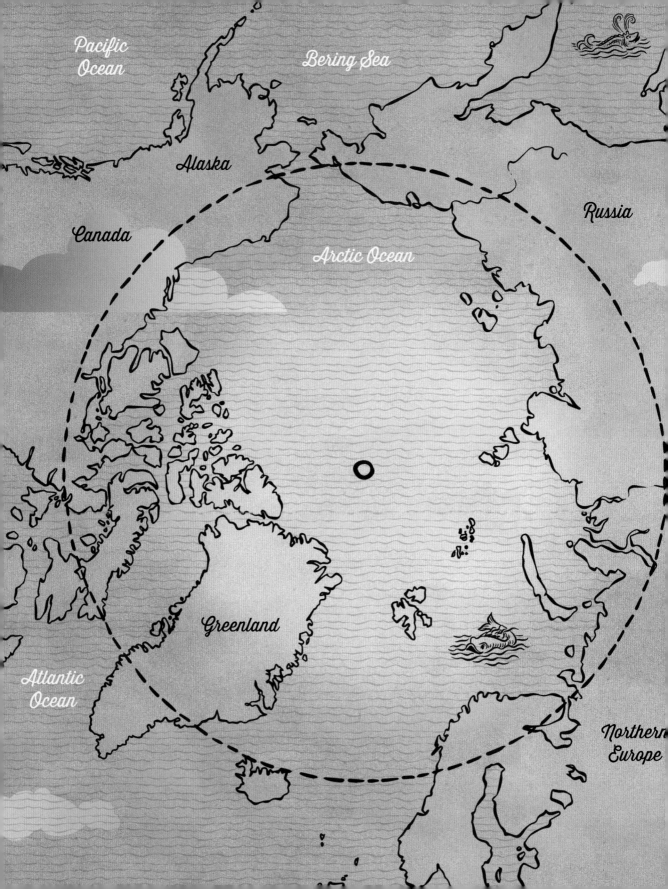

Chapter 6

First Contact

1,000 years ago

A PROPHECY COMES TRUE

★ The Thule of the Arctic and the Vikings

★ First contact between the people of North America and Europeans

The Prophecy

Quetzalcoatl was the Aztec god and founding king. One day the Evil Ones, the destroyers, came. One of the Evil Ones danced with bells on his ankles. His dancing and his singing stirred up the people. In mad revelry they gathered on a bridge. The bridge gave way, and all the people drowned.

The Evil One went into Quetzalcoatl's palace holding a mirror. It was a false mirror. When Quetzalcoatl looked at himself in it, instead of his own reflection he saw a bearded, long-faced person. He knew that if his people saw him like that, they would be terrified. He had no choice but to leave. On the eastern shore he set fire to himself. From then on, he was called the Lord of the Dawn. He rose each morning in the eastern sky. People gathered by the shore, waiting for him to return.

The prophecy that pale strangers with beards would arrive from the east one day is not only part of the complex Aztec myth system. It also appears in ancient myths across North America. The prophecy came true. Bearded strangers did come from the east.

THE ARCTIC IS A PLACE that tests anyone who lives there. The sun doesn't set in the summer, and the dark of night lasts all winter. For eight to ten months of the year the temperature is far below freezing. It can be minus 40 degrees for days on end.

Around 1,000 years ago the people archaeologists call Thule, who were the ancestors of modern Inuit, spread out of Alaska. They used

This Inuksuk stands in Rankin Inlet, Nunavut. It is one of many that are landmarks in the far North.

kayaks and umiaks for travel in open water and to hunt animals as large as the bowhead whale, which, at 15 to 18 m (50 to 60 feet) long and weighing up to a whopping 100 t (110 tons), is the largest animal in the Arctic seas.

The bowhead whale was like a general store for the necessities of life. Thule people had a use for every part of it. They made their shelters from its bones, they ate its meat, and they used its fat to make oil for cooking and heating. Even the baleen, the webbing in its mouth, was woven into baskets.

A bowhead whale

Thule hunters could travel fast in their large skin-covered boats or in sleds pulled by their dogs. Within a space of only 200 years, they had made their way east from Alaska right across the Arctic to northern Greenland, a distance of over 3,000 km (1,864 miles). When they got there, they met other people. One group they called Tuniit looked like the Thule, but they did not use boats or dogsleds. The Tuniit looked very strange because of their light skin and the light hair that even grew on their faces.

THE FIRST ARCTIC DWELLERS
The Tuniit

5,000 years ago

The Arctic was probably the last place to be inhabited in North America because it was covered by the Ice Age's ice fields longer than the rest of North America—in fact, ice still covers most of Greenland. Scientists propose that the Tuniit were the first people in the Arctic, and that they appeared first in Siberia around 7,000 years ago. They brought a new technology with them: the bow and arrow. The bow and arrow spread quickly across the Americas, but the Tuniit actually stopped relying on this weapon when they changed their focus from country foods like caribou to seafood like fish and seals. They didn't have boats, so they did their hunting from the edge of the ice, where a toggling harpoon is much more effective.

Almost everything else we know about the Tuniit comes from oral history preserved by modern Inuit. They tell about an ancient race of fine hunters who were taller than they were, and so strong that they could lift a boulder no Inuit would be able to budge. A single Tuniit man was said to be strong enough to crush the neck of a walrus with one arm and bring it home by himself across the ice.

An Inuit family rests at home after a successful seal hunt. Every bit of the seals will be used for food, clothing, and shelter.

The Story of Sedna

First, there were giants.

One day, as winter approached, two giants had a girl child. They called her Sedna. As the days got shorter, Sedna got bigger. Soon she was bigger than her mother and father. She was so big that there wasn't enough food for her to eat. She was so hungry she tried biting her parents.

That wouldn't do, so her parents pushed her into a canoe, and by the light of the moon they paddled out to sea. They heaved her into the ocean to drown. They felt awful about what they had done, but they thought that was the last of Sedna. They were wrong.

They had just started home when the canoe stopped. Sedna was holding their canoe and rocking it. If they couldn't stop her, she might climb back into the boat or tip the canoe.

Sedna's mother and father started to chop off her fingers. Each chopped-off finger became an animal: one became a whale, one became a seal, one a walrus, and one a salmon.

Sedna swam to the bottom of the sea, where she lives to this day. When the people are hungry they ask Sedna to send them more food, and she always does.

Stories about Sedna tell us that the icy Arctic waters have always fed the people of the North. The Thule took the place of the Tuniit, the first people to live in the Arctic, most likely by intermarrying and absorbing them into their own way of life.

Abraham Anghik Ruben's soapstone carving of Sedna and the Raven. Sedna is the goddess of sea animals in Inuit mythology.

THE VIKINGS

793 to 1055 CE

The first of the long-faced, bearded strangers of so many myths were most likely the Vikings. The Vikings sailed Europe's seas and rivers to trade and for conquest. History has labeled them ferocious raiders. They certainly would have been daunting enemies.

The Vikings reached Greenland at the same time as the Thule people. The first-ever European descriptions of North America come from the Norse *Saga of the Greenlanders* and *Erik the Red's Saga*. Written down in the early thirteenth century, the sagas were the only evidence that the Vikings had ever come to North America until 1960, when Anne Stine and her husband, Helge Ingstad, discovered the remains of a Viking settlement at L'Anse aux Meadows, Newfoundland.

In 2015 advances in remote-sensing techniques using infrared images from 644 km (400 miles) up in space helped scientists find traces of another settlement at Point Rosee, on the southwest coast of Newfoundland.

This reconstruction of the Viking village at L'Anse aux Meadows shows the sod walls and roofs of the buildings. The village included houses and workshops for the iron smithy, carpenters, and for boat repairs.

Boatloads of Vikings settled with their sheep and cattle. They even built a cathedral, and a bishop was appointed for Greenland. The clothing and jewelry the Vikings left behind look like the belongings of prosperous farmers, not of sailors or warriors come to pillage. Clearly, they intended to stay.

But they didn't stay.

The weather had turned very cold again in the late 1300s, but cold alone wouldn't have been enough to discourage the hardy Vikings. Their sagas describe violent conflicts with the Skraelings (the Norse term for the Thule) in Newfoundland and elsewhere. We don't know what really happened. We do know that the Vikings abandoned their dreams to settle permanently in North America. Around 1340 they started their retreat to Iceland and Europe. The first contact between these two peoples ended with some of the fiercest, most capable Europeans driven back across the sea.

Viking ships were fast and strong, even in very shallow water. Ships were so important to the Vikings that they appear on jewelry, monuments, and coins. Some people were even buried in ships, or in tombs that looked like ships.

ARCHAEOLOGICAL TOOL:
Infrared Technology

Archaeologists are beginning to use satellites with infrared survey capabilities to help them "see" changes in the earth's surface. Infrared light has a longer wavelength than the visible light we can see. What appear are patterns created by the way light reflects off different plants that grow when soil is disturbed by digging to build houses or yards. Ground-penetrating radar is another technique that archaeologists can use to construct a three-dimensional image to show where human-made structures are buried, even if they lie beneath the soil and vegetation. With this useful method, archaeologists can precisely determine where to dig rather than disturbing the whole site.

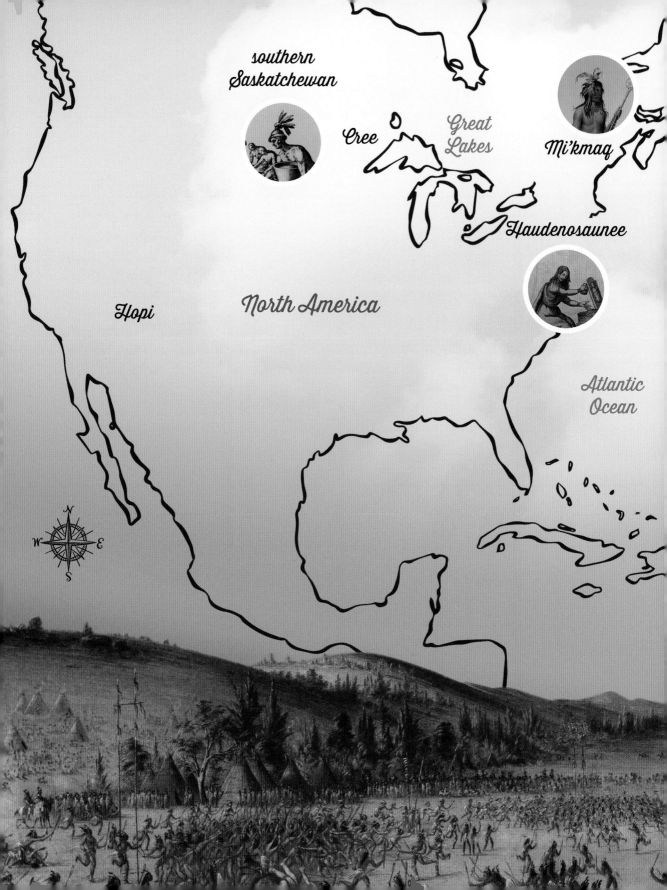

southern
Saskatchewan

Cree

Great
Lakes

Mi'kmaq

Haudenosaunee

Hopi

North America

Atlantic
Ocean

Chapter 7

In the Year 1491

THE LAST SUMMER
Take part in a trade fair:

★ Watch solemn diplomacy at work

★ Enjoy new foods

★ See old friends and make new ones as you sing,
dance, and play games together

In 1491, the year before Christopher Columbus set out across the sea to what he thought was India, North America was a dynamic and complex place.

A TIME FOR VARIETY

In 1491 there was no such thing as a single way of life. Hundreds of different groups lived in North America, each with their own way of doing things. For instance, you could find people living in enormous wooden longhouses, tepees made of skins and wooden poles, and houses made of adobe brick. There was plenty of variety in food, too. You could feast on dozens of foods from succotash to oysters, from strawberries to smoked salmon. Fashions were different depending on where you lived. You could hear more than 2,000 different languages spoken.

The importance of community for the Haudenosaunee is reflected in their longhouses, home to up to twenty families. Often two families shared a hearth.

A TIME FOR RITUAL

The people of North America led rich spiritual lives and practiced rituals that expressed their beliefs. Here is just a sample of the rituals you might have taken part in if you lived in 1491:

Dancers at Grand Canyon Park in 2011

Drawing of traditional ballplayers

A TIME FOR STORYTELLING

On the Atlantic coast you could hear a Mi'kmaq storyteller beating on a drum or log to signal that storytelling was about to begin. People of all ages gathered eagerly to listen to funny stories, scary stories, and many that mixed humor, horror, and life lessons. The stories were easy to remember and pass on to new generations.

An Excerpt from "Muin, the Bear's Child"

Sigo's father died when he was just a baby. His mother remarried, but Sigo's new stepfather was jealous of the little boy. He came up with a scheme to get rid of Sigo. He told his wife that he would take the child hunting.

The stepfather took Sigo to a dark cave. Sigo was afraid to go in, but his stepfather shoved him. Once Sigo was in the cave, his stepfather blocked the opening with a boulder, trapping the boy. The man planned to go to the beach at Blomidon but to tell everybody that he had been looking for Sigo.

Glooscap could see into the man's heart, and he was very angry. As the stepfather walked along the beach, Glooscap caused the ground to split. The man was buried under falling rocks.

Glooscap sent his servant Matues the porcupine to Sigo. Matues called to the other animals to help, but they could not budge the rock sealing the cave.

Muin'iskw, the she-bear, heard the noise and left the woods to help. She was able to move the rock. Sigo was very young and needed somebody to take care of him. That is how Muin'iskw became his godmother.

GLOOSCAP

Glooscap is a cultural hero who appears often in Mi'kmaq oral tradition. He brought people into being, but he was also a trickster. Many stories about Glooscap describe him granting a wish to selfish people, only to watch the unexpected results.

Statue at the Glooscap Heritage Centre in Nova Scotia

A TIME FOR HARVEST FESTIVALS

In the woodlands around the Great Lakes, you could take part in ceremonies of the Haudenosaunee that recognized the gift of agriculture. To give thanks to the Great Spirit for the earth's bounty, six major festivals took place during the year: Maple, Planting, Strawberry, Green Corn, Harvest, and Midwinter or New Year.

Festivals meant feasts. Haudenosaunee women prepare food while a baby on a cradleboard watches. Cradleboards were a way for babies to be kept safe and comfortable.

A TIME FOR DANCING

In the Southwest, Katsinas, good-natured spirits from the underworld that looked more or less like humans, came to Hopi village plazas, where they danced and were fed spirit food (cornmeal). In exchange, they would ask the gods to let the rain come.

A TIME FOR SPORTS

Games like lacrosse and double ball built strength and community spirit but also acted as ritualized battles to settle disputes. The games strengthened diplomatic alliances and, most important, honored the Great Spirit. The most thrilling game of all was lacrosse. Lacrosse was played by many nations east of the Mississippi River to the Atlantic Ocean and north into what is now Canada. In fact, it's now Canada's official summer sport.

From 100 to 10,000 players were on the field at any one time—and that doesn't include all the spectators. Their bodies and faces painted to look fierce, the men—women didn't take part—played games lasting several days on playing fields that were the huge open spaces between villages.

Running between goalposts, which could be rocks or trees, spaced anywhere from 457 m (1,500 feet) to several miles apart kept the players fit and strong, but that wasn't the only reason they played. They played for the enjoyment of the Great Powers. Today, members of the Onandaga Nation still call lacrosse the Creator's game.

Lacrosse players, accompanied by shamans, spent the summer running, tumbling, and tossing a ball to get ready for the autumn games. In some places they ate a special diet in preparation, avoiding eating rabbits (which might make them too timid), frogs (so their bones wouldn't become brittle like a frog's), or certain fish (which could make them too sluggish). And they avoided having anything to do with women.

We pitisowewepahikan (Cree for "double ball") was one of the games played by women. The players had to be in top condition because the playing field could be very large, and the action was fast and rough. Two goals were marked out, at the east and west ends of the field. Two deerskin pouches were stuffed with buffalo hair or sand and joined by a leather thong—this was the ball. Two teams lined up facing each other, each woman holding a stick about 0.9 m (3 feet) long. To start the game, the ball was thrown up in the air. The players would try to catch the thong on their stick. The ball moved down the field, tossed from one player's stick to another, like a mixture of modern hockey and soccer. The player who tossed the ball through the opposite team's goalpost scored a goal. Of course, the other team did everything possible to intercept the ball or unhook it from an opponent's stick.

Artist George Catlin drew many pictures of people living on the Great Plains in the 1830s and 1840s. Catlin's depiction of Choctaw ballplayers from 1844 shows the many players involved in the game.

A TIME FOR DIPLOMACY

The year 1491 was a time for skillful diplomacy because people were coming together in new alliances. The population was growing quickly thanks to abundant corn crops. People were living in larger settlements: around the Lower Great Lakes there were towns of 2,000 people or more. When this many people live together, there have to be rules, and somebody has to make decisions. There were religious leaders who under-stood sacred rituals, leaders who could settle disputes, and military leaders who took charge in times of battle. In 1491, leaders were actively forging alliances, and new nations were forming.

One such alliance was the Haudenosaunee Confederacy. We don't know the exact date when five nations—the Mohawk, Oneida, Onondaga, Cayuga, and Seneca—came together to form the Haudenosaunee Confederacy (sometimes called the Iroquois Confederacy) to live in harmony, but many believe it is a model for the Constitution of the United States.

Several large villages flourished on what is now called Manhattan Island. This village is made up of a dozen longhouses, each housing several families, and would have been typical in 1491.

TRADE FAIRS
A Time for Coming Together

Trade, stately diplomacy, and rowdy fun all came together in trade fairs. Think about a busy shopping mall, a raucous rock concert, and a dignified meeting of heads of state all rolled into one, and you will get a sense of the excitement of a trade fair.

Dances have always been an important part of Indigenous life. People danced to give thanks, to ensure a successful hunt, or to bring about a good harvest. In the picture, the artist shows a medicine dance taking place in a longhouse.

The two villages in what is now southern Saskatchewan were different. One was home to the Nakoda, people who hunted bison. The other was home to farmers, who lived in a village made of earthen houses and tended fields where they grew crops.

In the past, the two peoples had gotten along well, but lately there had been bad blood between them. It started with a raid, and then there was a murder, and then some of the farmers' crops were trampled. Something had to be done to make peace before things got worse.

They decided to hold a trade fair. There was no better way to patch up differences. At first, they feared that another fight would break out over where the fair should be held. Finally, they picked a spot in the Souris River Valley between the feuding villages. It was a good choice. There was plenty of wood to fuel cooking fires and a good source of fresh water for drinking and washing. Lots of wood and water would be needed because thousands of people would camp there for days.

The heart of every trade fair was a solemn ceremony where differences could be settled peacefully. On the first day of the fair, a canopy was set up in the center of the campground. Everybody gathered to witness the ceremony. The village leader made a pile of spears, clubs, bows and arrows, pottery, and jewelry. On top of it he placed a large pipe with a red stone bowl and a long flat stem. Then the Nakoda leader took his turn to make a pile. He topped it with the skull of a buffalo. The piles of goods were exchanged.

When the formal trading was over, the rift was mended.

In what is now Florida, men transport fruits and vegetables to the communal storehouses, to be shared by everyon

After all the formalities were over, there was plenty of lively informal trading, too. You could go home with cloudy-colored chert (like brown flint) blades as sharp as razors all the way from the coast of Labrador, a basket full of dried salmon from the West Coast, prairie turnips from the Plains, and pemmican made of deer and moose meat from around the Great Lakes. You could find a pouch of seeds for a new kind of corn or squash or beans to plant, and get advice from the trader who brought them to the fair from the Southwest.

The ceremonies and the trade were serious business. But for most people, going to a trade fair also meant having a wonderful time. It was a time for friendship. Old friends caught up on gossip and news. Young people showed off new hairstyles and tattoos, and they displayed their skill at all kinds of games. Romantic couples looked for quiet spots to be alone, while noisy crowds bet on the men who put on sleight-of-hand competitions, and the women rolling dice. Musicians wandered through the campground playing their flutes.

Feasts were held under the night skies, and the dancing, singing, and storytelling went on until dawn.

Nobody knew that everything was about to change.

Getting ready for a feast was a lot of work. Several cooks work together to prepare, sort, and boil corn to be eaten at a community celebration.

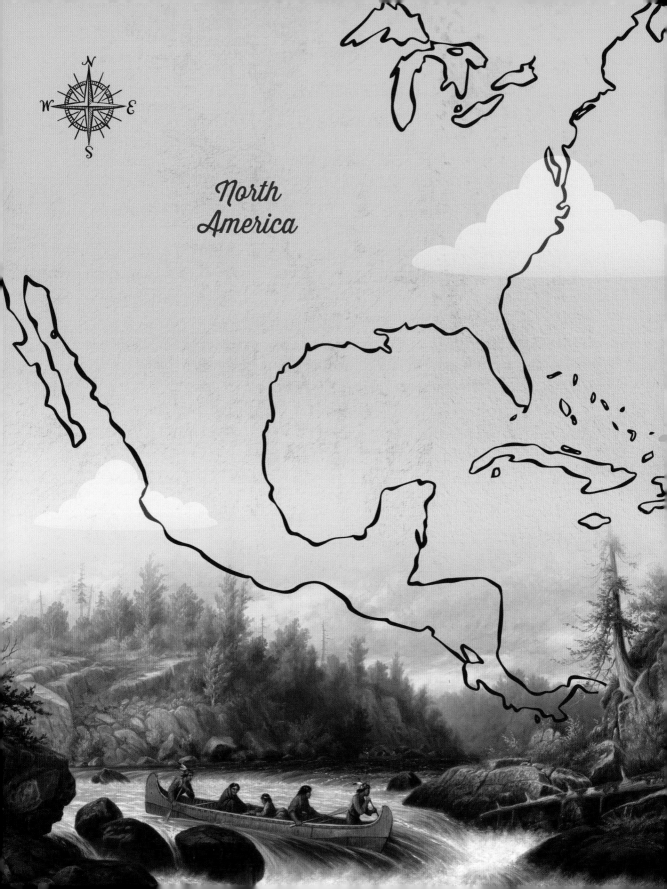

North America

Chapter 8

After the End of the World

1492 to the present

THE CIRCLE IS BROKEN

FROM THE **OGLALA SIOUX TRADITION**

The Power of the Circle

Everything in the world is a circle. The nests of birds are built in circles. Tepees are round, and they are set in circles. Every person's life is a circle that leads from childhood back to childhood. There is great power in the circle.

CENTURIES OF CALAMITY threaten the circle of life.

Christopher Columbus sailed west in four voyages between 1492 and 1508, looking for Asian gold and treasures to take home to Spain. Columbus never got to Asia, and he never set foot in North America either (he landed on Caribbean islands), but he opened the way for Europeans to claim that they had found a "new world." The Spaniards were the first of waves of Europeans who came, hungry for gold and glory, and determined to convert souls to Christianity.

More than five centuries have passed since Columbus first wrote, "They are the best people in the world," and then went on to enslave and murder the people he met when he arrived in the Americas.

The circle of life that had sustained millions of people was broken by disease, slavery, war, forced resettlement, and assimilation.

Columbus's ships, the *Nina*, the *Pinta*, and the *Santa Maria*, sail across the Atlantic Ocean, in search of India and its spices and other riches. When they landed, they mistakenly thought they had reached India.

THE RAGE OF MANITOU

The man was born in a village by the Atlantic. He was only seven when British sailors captured him and sold him as a slave in Spain. He escaped to England with the help of the priests who rescued him. When he got there, he found a place to stay in the home of a shipbuilder. His job was to be a living curiosity—a souvenir to show off to the shipbuilder's gawking guests. Considering the times, his "host" treated him well. He taught the man English and eventually helped him find passage on a ship sailing to Newfoundland.

Once the man landed, he thought his troubles were over. He got a berth on a boat that was supposed to be going south to his home. Instead, the ship's captain changed his mind. The man found himself crossing the Atlantic again.

Eventually he got back to New England. As he stood on the deck to get a look at the coast, he saw a horrifying sight. The shore was empty. Utterly empty. When he had left, one bustling village after another lined the water. Now there was nothing but tangled shrubs that had reclaimed the old villages for the forest. The only signs that human beings had ever lived there were skeletons, lying on the shore, bleached by the sun.

This is a true story. The people at Plymouth knew the man as Tisquantum, but that wasn't his real name. Where he was from, the word meant "rage of Manitou." Manitou was the Great Spirit, the life force who gave the land to the people. Manitou had reason to rage when he saw what had happened to his people.

DISEASE
Smallpox

How could a handful of Spanish sailors and soldiers do such dreadful damage to people who were able to adapt to vastly different environments and build cities, seasoned traders who knew how to negotiate despite differences in customs and languages, and who had managed to turn away the fierce Vikings?

When the Spanish landed, they brought along guns and pigs. Spanish guns were no match for any good archer. The guns were inaccurate and so slow to load that an archer could make speedy work of somebody fumbling with one. Devastation came from something the Spanish didn't even know they and their pigs were bringing: germs.

The Spanish invaders can rightly be charged with many evil things, but not with deliberately spreading disease. In the fifteenth and early sixteenth centuries, nobody in the world knew what a germ was. The microscope wouldn't be invented until 1590. Edward Jenner would discover a vaccine for smallpox only in 1798, more than 300 years after Columbus sailed from Europe.

Of course, everyone dies of something. People in North America suffered from their share of diseases just as they did all over the world. Infections, arthritis, tuberculosis, cancer, and syphilis were familiar afflictions. But this wave of disease was different. People in North America had no immunity to diseases such as measles, smallpox, and influenza. Nobody had the vaccines to protect them against these awful diseases, but the Europeans had built up immunities that protected them. By contrast, the Indigenous people were hit hard.

Not only the sick died. When the adults who hunted or tended the fields died, their children died of starvation. There were fewer animals to hunt anyway. The pigs that escaped when the Spanish landed had infected native animals like turkeys and other game the people depended on for food.

The trade routes that had played such an enormous part in daily life now played a terrible role in spreading diseases. For instance, smallpox takes ten days

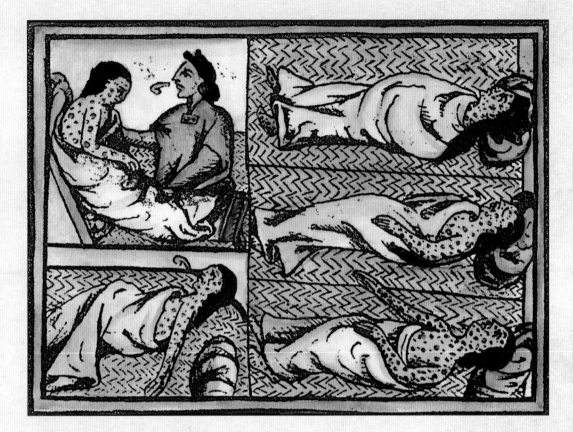

to appear. An infected trader could be far from home without realizing he was ill. He could infect villages where no one had even heard of the Spanish.

Smallpox was one of the diseases that devastated the people of North America. As late as 1967, two million people around the world died from it. Thanks to strong vaccination efforts around the world, it was declared wiped out in 1977.

Because nobody agrees on exactly how many people lived in North America before the Spanish came, nobody can ever know how many people died. Estimates set the number of dead as high as 95 percent of the population. That means that from a population that had once numbered in the millions, only 250,000 people were left by the beginning of the 1900s. It was the greatest disaster in all of human history.

SLAVERY

☞ In 1524, a child was kidnapped by explorers from Florence, Italy, and taken to be "displayed" in France. After that, Indigenous people were often enslaved to provide labor for European settlers.

☞ From around 1670, the French accepted slaves as gifts from Indigenous people who had captured members of enemy groups. Documents from the time describe enslaved Fox and Sioux from the western Great Lakes, Inuit from Labrador, Chickasaw from the Mississippi Valley, Apache from the American Southeast, and Pawnee from the Missouri Basin.

☞ African and Indigenous men, women, and children were sold at a slave market built at the foot of Wall Street in New York in 1709. In the 1752 census, 147 Indigenous slaves were listed as part of households in what became Illinois. When the Spanish settled in California in 1769, priests baptized whole villages and made the people relocate to missions, where they had to work voluntarily—or involuntarily. In 1850 An Act for the Government and Protection of Indians was passed, which meant, among other things, that Indigenous children could be indentured—forced to work as "apprentices."

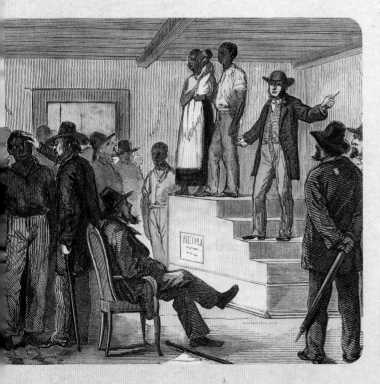

Kidnapped African men, women, and children were sold in markets like the one in this engraving from New York City.

WAR Indigenous people were not strangers to warfare, but life was drastically changed by two wars that had little to do with them. In the 1700s, explorers from France and Great Britain were sailing around the world searching for treasure. When they went to war against each other, those hostilities spread to North America. The French and English competed for the valuable fur trade. Indigenous people understood politics and alliances, so their military help was highly prized by both France and England in the French and Indian War (1754–1763) and in the American Revolution (1775–1783). These were two separate wars, but all they did was determine who would take power over Indigenous people.

The many battles that were fought between government troops and Indigenous people were extraordinarily vicious and bloody. Perhaps the most infamous was the Battle of Wounded Knee.

The Battle of Wounded Knee

In the United States, the Bureau of Indian Affairs (BIA) was worried. The Sioux were gathering on the prairies to perform the Ghost Dance, asking for advice from their ancestors and spirits so that they could survive the deprivation they were suffering as they were forced onto reservations after their food source, the buffalo, disappeared. (There were about 50 million of the animals on the Plains before the Europeans came. By the 1890s, they were all but extinct.)

Chief Sitting Bull was arrested on December 15, 1890, to put a stop to the Ghost Dances. The arrest turned violent, and Sitting Bull was killed. Another Oglala Sioux leader, Big Foot, was afraid of police retaliation, so in the dark of night he led his band south to find protection with Chief Red Cloud on the Pine Ridge Reservation.

Two weeks later, the US Seventh Cavalry found Big Foot's band. Hungry and exhausted, the men, women, and children were marched to Wounded Knee Creek. The following morning, the cavalry tried to take their weapons from them.

Nobody is sure what happened next on that cold morning, but a gun went off. Tragically, 487 US solders ringed the band and opened fire. When it was over, 256 Sioux lay dead.

The Oglala leader American Horse testified to the commissioner of Indian Affairs in 1891: "There was a woman with an infant in her arms who was killed as she almost touched the flag of truce . . . the child not knowing that its mother was dead was still nursing, and that was especially a very sad sight . . ."

Twenty of the soldiers got Congressional Medals of Honor for the slaughter at Wounded Knee.

US soldiers buried the bodies of the Oglala Sioux who died at the Battle of Wounded Knee in a common grave.

TORN FROM THE LAND

As more Europeans arrived in North America, they wanted more and more land. From 1830 to 1840, force and dozens of broken treaties drove Indigenous people from their ancestral lands. At least 90,000 Native Americans were made to leave their homes and move west of the Mississippi River. The move to separate people from their ancient homelands was relentless:

* In 1763, a Royal Proclamation was issued, establishing a firm western boundary for the British colonies in what is now Canada and the US. The rest of the land was called the "Indian Territories," and there could be no settlement there unless the Indian Department allowed it.

Oglala Sioux survivors of Wounded Knee wait for rations at the Pine Ridge Agency.

* After the American War of Independence, 30,000 United Empire Loyalists—colonists who were loyal to the British king—moved into what is now Canada. The Six Nations of the Iroquois Confederacy had fought alongside the British, so many Indigenous people also moved. Lands were "surrendered" by Indigenous people along the St. Lawrence River down to the Great Lakes to make room for the settlers.

* On January 12, 1833, a law was passed to prohibit any Indigenous person from staying within Florida state borders.

* In 1832, federal troops herded the Cherokee into camps where they were imprisoned because they wouldn't move west; 1,500 died. The rest were forced on a 1,287-km (800-mile) march, the Trail of Tears, to Oklahoma in the fall. In all, 4,000 Cherokee died in the process of being torn from their land.

* In 1864, Kit Carson led government men in forcing 8,000 Navajo to walk more than 482 km (300 miles) from their ancestral land to a new reservation at barren, desolate Bosque Redondo in northwestern New Mexico. In 1868, the Navajo were allowed to return home—if they promised to stay on their reservations and become ranchers and farmers.

* In 1890, Congress established the Oklahoma Territory on Indian Territory, breaking a sixty-year-old pledge to preserve the area for Native Americans forced from their land in the east.

* In 1953, over 100 tribes were "terminated": they were made subject to state laws, and their land was sold to non-Indians.

ASSIMILATION

Many of those who came to North America from Great Britain or other European countries were convinced that European culture was superior.

They sincerely believed that they would be doing Indigenous people good if they could convert them to Christianity, teach them to farm, and give them an education based on reading, writing, and arithmetic. They wanted to assimilate Indigenous people—to make them just like themselves. Either they didn't realize or didn't care that Indigenous people had their own religions, had known how to farm (and hunt and fish) for thousands of years, and had their own ways of educating children. Even when it was well-intentioned, the cost of assimilation was that people were expected to abandon the ways of life that had served them well for so long.

From around 1820, the government of what is now Canada tried different ways to "assimilate" Indigenous people. One early experiment happened at Coldwater-Narrows near Lake Simcoe in Ontario. A group of Ojibwa were supposed to settle in a "model" village—that meant it was just like the settlers' villages—where they could live just like the newcomers from Britain. Of course, it didn't work. Nevertheless, the Canadian government kept up the policy for 150 years.

The Coldwater-Narrows Model Village, built like a settler village, was supposed to make Ojibwa people live like British newcomers, including wearing the same clothes.

Residential Schools

How better to assimilate people than by education? In 1879, the first group of eighty-four Lakota children arrived at the new United States Indian Training and Industrial School at Carlisle, Pennsylvania. It was a boarding school designed to remove young people from their own culture and remake them as members of the larger society. Soon there were 24 such schools, 81 boarding schools, and 150 day schools in the United States.

The Indian Act in Canada gave authority over Indigenous people to the federal Department of Indian Affairs. They could even decide who was an Indian. Canadian public policy in 1883 was focused on creating residential schools for "civilization" and "assimilation." Indian children were to have the same education as the rest of Canada, but at a cost: they were not allowed to speak their own languages, they couldn't wear traditional clothing, they couldn't practice their ancient religions, and because Canada is large, they were forced to leave their parents and homes to attend distant schools. Those who resisted were punished, sometimes brutally. Between 1857 and 1996, there were 132 residential schools in Canada. In all, 150,000 children attended them.

Girls and the nun who is their teacher in a classroom at Cross Lake Indian Residential School in Manitoba in 1940.

A boy named Thomas Moore, before and after he was sent to the Regina Indian Residential School in Saskatchewan in 1874.

Girls taking part in "ironing class" at the Carlisle Indian School in Pennsylvania, around 1901.

North America

Chapter 9

Healing the Circle

to the future

GHOST DANCERS RISE

At the 500th anniversary of Columbus's landing, tribal leaders gathered in Washington, DC, for a ceremony in front of the Capitol. They could have dwelt on the catastrophes that were Columbus's legacy, but instead they closed the ceremony with these words:

> *We stand young warriors*
> *In the circle*
> *At dawn all storm clouds disappear*
> *The future brings all hope and glory,*
> *Ghost dancers rise*
> *Five-hundred years.*

POVERTY AND LOSS

This is a story of almost unimaginable tragedy. Indigenous people looking back on the five centuries since the European invasion began to know what comes after the end of the world. Their ancestors' lives and culture were ended due to war, disease, and starvation. The impact of colonization continues to influence Indigenous peoples' lives. Over the past several hundred years, their lands, resources, and livelihoods have been taken away or destroyed. With few ways to make a living and to feel purpose and a connection to the world at large, they struggle to create thriving and healthy communities.

A GREAT SILENCE

With so few people speaking them now, most Indigenous languages are in danger of disappearing forever. People transmit culture through language, so when a language is lost, the result is a loss of traditional knowledge and of the stories and myths that were vital to a people's understanding of the world. What follows are generations unsure of their culture and disconnected from their identity.

At the start of the twentieth century, the population of the Indigenous peoples of North America was dropping fast due to aggressive warfare and colonization in the nineteenth century. Anthropologists assumed they would eventually vanish, and urgently studied their cultures. But the dire predictions did not come true.

A Cree man speaks at a Canada Day powwow on Princes Island, Alberta.

A NEW KIND OF ADAPTATION

Ancient people survived because one generation taught skills to the next, such as flint-knapping to make stone tools, which were useful for adapting to new environments. Like their ancestors, Indigenous people nowadays are adjusting to an unfamiliar world. Instead of bows and arrows, they are using computer skills to create a brighter future. However, many of their ancient discoveries (foods such as corn, plants such as tobacco, and technology such as rubber) still appear in our daily life. As citizens of this world, they continue to make contributions in the arts and sciences just as their ancestors did. Through both individual and collective actions, Indigenous people are determined to be vibrant members of modern society and to leave their mark on it.

A Cree designer shares her ideas on a whiteboard.

LIVING IN A MULTICULTURAL LAND

Today Indigenous peoples are a fast-growing population. However, they are only one minority in a multicultural nation. Ancient America was also a multicultural place, with diverse peoples across the continent practicing unique customs and speaking many different languages. When the idea of "Indians" formed in the minds of Europeans, it tended to obscure the cultural diversity that existed. In fact, there was never just one "Indian nation." There was never one leader who could speak for the many distinct communities occupying the continent. However, Indigenous leaders now recognize the benefits of speaking with a single unified voice. They see the advantages of combining their energies to achieve their political goals in the nations that dominate North America today.

WE, THE INDIGENOUS PEOPLES

In the twentieth century, organizations such as the Assembly of First Nations (AFN) in Canada and the National Congress of the American Indian (NCAI) in the United States were created by Indigenous people to interact with the national governments and the United Nations. The leaders of these groups are elected to bring a unified voice to political action—for example, when the topic is education. At other times they might seek the attention of local governments to support arts and culture in their communities.

RECLAIMING A HOMELAND

The coat of arms of Nunavut

Inuit were once a people isolated by geography. As recently as the 1950s, many of them still lived on the land in much the same way their ancestors did. In 1999, they changed the map of Canada when an area of land called Nunavut was made a formal territory of the country through negotiation and a referendum. Like the Inuit in Greenland, the Inuit in Nunavut have achieved a form of home rule that gives them local control of government. The Inuit Tapiriit Kanatami is the political organization that represents the interests of Inuit people across Arctic Canada.

NEW PATHS TO SUCCESS AND CHANGE

Professional athlete is one career that has replaced the warrior path for Indigenous men. Like the ancient Olmec ballplayers, athletes can exercise their physical talents and gain prestige. Although there were famous Indigenous athletes such as Jim Thorpe and Tom Longboat early in the twentieth century, they were few and far between. As we begin a new century, professional sports, especially hockey in Canada, is a realistic goal for athletes from First Nations. Names such as Jonathon Cheechoo, Brandon Montour, Jordin Tootoo, Jordan Nolan, and Carey Price are just some of the Indigenous men who are players in the National Hockey League.

Artistic traditions were and are as varied as the people and the languages they spoke. Some customs, such as carving totem poles, never faded and have become popular symbols of the West Coast. In ancient times, only Arctic peoples saw inuksuit, but today the stone men of the North that once aided in the caribou hunt appear everywhere across North America. When Vancouver, BC, hosted the 2010 Winter Olympics, the games' emblem, Ilaanaq, was inspired by an inukshuk.

Some expressive arts are unique to modern times, but they still communicate the artists' vision through their works.

Singers such as Buffy Sainte-Marie (Cree) and Robbie Robertson (Haudenosaunee) helped define the revolutionary sound in the early days of rock-and-roll music. Today, both are past seventy years old, and they continue to produce new music for audiences to enjoy. Their talent inspired a new generation of musicians, such as Tanya Tagaq (Inuit) and the band A Tribe Called Red (whose members are Haudenosaunee and Anishnaabe) from Ottawa, Ontario, to transform traditional singing into contemporary music.

From top to bottom:
Actor Adam Beach
Singer and songwriter Buffy Sainte-Marie
Rock legend Robbie Robertson
Los Angeles Kings center Jordan Nolan

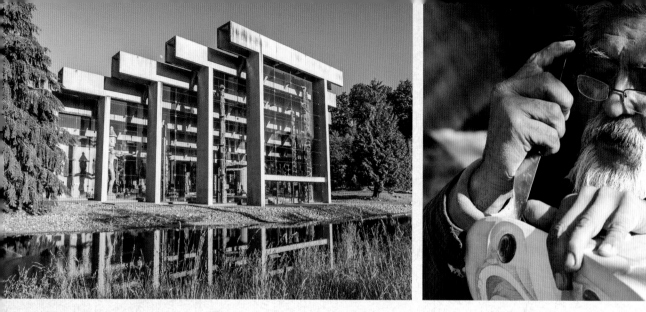

The Museum of Anthropology at the University of British Columbia

A carver works on yellow cedar Eagle piece.

Visual artists such as Daphne Odjig (Anishnaabe) and Bill Reid (Haida) looked to their traditional cultures to create artwork that made them famous internationally. They created a legacy for younger artists such as Shelley Niro (Haudenosaunee) and Susan Point (Musqueam), whose works appear in public spaces such as museums and airports.

Although writing is a recent addition to the Indigenous cultures of North America, authors such as Wab Kinew and Sherman Alexie have received many awards for their writing.

THE POWWOW
A Modern Tradition with Ancient Roots

Among Indigenous people today, *powwow* refers to a popular public celebration that includes singing, showy dancing while wearing regalia, rodeos, parades, craft fairs, and pancake breakfasts. Powwows encourage people to express the spirit of their cultures. Since the city lifestyle is now typical for many Indigenous people, these community festivals are often a highlight of summer travel plans. Powwow season is the best time to return to their nations and visit friends and family.

Dancers take part in the Julyamsh powwow in Coeur d'Alene, Idaho.

The steps performed in modern powwow dancing, and the style of singing ~e originally customs among the peoples of the Plains. Powwows be common across the United States after World War II. The Blackfeet of Browning, Montana, celebrated their first North American Indian Days with a powwow in 1953. In Canada, the Piikani Nation hosted the first powwow in 1954 in their village of Brocket, Alberta. They borrowed elements from their culture that used to be dedicated to religious ceremonies and feasting. The powwow is a public event that honors community spirit.

ORIGINS OF DANCING

Piikani storytellers recall that long ago, shortly after the world was created, the hunts were unsuccessful and people were hungry. A wolf pack that lived in the sky country saw their plight and felt sorry for them. They came down to teach the people skills that would help them thrive. Their last gift to the ancestors was the style of singing that sky wolves howled in their celebrations. Then they returned to the sky country by their Wolf Road, which we still see at night—we call it the Milky Way. As people began singing they also wanted to dance, so they learned from the animals. Depending on the rhythm of the drum and the songs that go along with the beat, dancers will perform the owl dance, the prairie chicken dance, or the crow hop.

LOOKING TO THE FUTURE

While the twenty-first century is still young, it will be remarkably different for Indigenous peoples. President Obama signed the Native American Apology Resolution in December 2009 on behalf of the people of the United States. However, the resolution remains unknown to most people because no public declaration about it was made. Since Canada's Truth and Reconciliation Commission, studying the impact of residential schools, issued its final report in June 2015, there is an opportunity to create new relationships in Canada. For the first time in a long, long time, Indigenous people can dream of a better life and work toward a better future.

Children celebrate at the Echoes of a Proud Nation Pow Wow in Kahnawake, Quebec

SELECTED SOURCES

Books:

Adovasio J. M. and Jake Page. *The First Americans: In Pursuit of Archaeology's Greatest Mystery*. New York: Modern Library, 2003.

Black Elk and John G. Niehardt. *Black Elk Speaks: Being the Life Story of a Holy Man of the Oglala Sioux*. Winnipeg: Bison Books, 2004. First published as *Black Elk Speaks* in 1932.

Dillehay, Tom. *Monte Verde: A Late Pleistocene Settlement in Chile*. Washington, DC: Smithsonian Institution Scholarly Press, 1989.

Fedje, Daryl and Rolf Mathewes. *Haida Gwaii: Human History and Environment from the Time of Loon to the Time of the Iron People*. Vancouver: UBC Press, 2005.

Josephy, Alvin M., Jr. *500 Nations: An Illustrated History of North American Indians*. New York: Alfred A. Knopf, 1994.

Mann, Charles C. *1491: New Revelations of the Americas Before Columbus*. New York: Vintage Books, 2005.

McGhee, Robert. *Ancient People of the Arctic*. Vancouver: UBC Press, 1996.

McMillan, Alan D. and Eldon Yellowhorn. *First Peoples in Canada*. Vancouver: Douglas & McIntyre, 2004.

Page, Jake. *In the Hands of the Great Spirit: The 20,000-Year History of American Indians*. New York: Free Press, 2003.

Wright, J. V. *A History of the Native People of Canada, Volume 1*. Ottawa: Canadian Museum of Civilization, 1996.

Journals and Articles:

Baltus, Melissa R. and Sarah E. Baires. Elements of Ancient Power in the Cahokian World. *Journal of Social Archaeology* 12(2): 167–192, 2012.

Boldurian, Anthony T. Clovis Type-Site, Blackwater Draw, New Mexico: A History, 1929–2009. *North American Archaeologist*, 29(1): 65–89, 2008.

Dillehay, Tom D. A Late Ice-Age Settlement in Southern Chile. *Scientific American* 251(4):106–117, 1984.

Figgins, J. D. An Additional Discovery of the Association of a "Folsom" Artifact and Fossil Mammal Remains. *Proceedings of the Colorado Museum of Natural History*, 10(4): 23–24, 1931.

Fladmark, K. R. Routes: Alternate Migration Corridors for Early Man in North America. *American Antiquity* 44(1): 55–69, 1979.

Haines, Helen R., David G. Smith, David Galbraith, and Tys Theysmeyer. The Point of Popularity: A Summary of 10,000 Years of Human Activity at the Princess Point Promontory, Cootes Paradise Marsh, Hamilton, Ontario. *Canadian Journal of Archaeology* 35(2): 232–257, 2011.

Ludwin, Ruth S., Robert Dennis, Deborah Carver, Alan D. McMillan, Robert Losey, John Clague, Chris Jonientz-Trisler, Janine Bowechop, Jacilee Wray, and Karen James. Dating the 1700 Cascadia Earthquake: Great Coastal Earthquakes in Native Stories. *Seismological Research Letters*, 76(2): 140–148, 2005.

Zeder, Melinda A. Central Questions in the Domestication of Plants and Animals. *Evolutionary Anthropology*, 15(3): 105–117, 2006.

Websites:

Canadian Museum of History, Gatineau, Quebec
www.historymuseum.ca

Museum of Anthropology, Mexico City
www.mna.inah.gob.mx

National Museum of the American Indian, part of the Smithsonian Institute in Washington, D.C.
www.nmai.si.edu

FURTHER READING

Hakim, Joy. *A History of US: The First Americans: Prehistory–1600.* New York: Oxford University Press, 2007.

Ipellie, Alootook and David MacDonald. *The Inuit Thought of It: Amazing Arctic Innovations.* Toronto: Annick Press, 2007.

Landon, Rocky and David MacDonald. *A Native American Thought of It: Amazing Inventions and Innovations.* Toronto: Annick Press, 2008.

Ortiz, Simon. *The People Shall Continue.* San Francisco: Children's Book Press, 1997.

Sigafus, Kim and Lyle Ernst. *Wisdom from Our First Nations.* Toronto: Second Story Press, 2015.

IMAGE CREDITS

CHAPTER 4: 42 (top) National Geographic Creative / Alamy Stock Photo; (center) World History Archive / Alamy Stock Photo; (bottom) Granger Historical Picture Archive / Alamy Stock Photo; 44 (icon) SKARIDA / Shutterstock.com; 45 National Geographic Creative / Alamy Stock Photo; 46 World History Archive / Alamy Stock Photo; 47 (top) Microgen / Shutterstock.com; (bottom) Bill Whittaker / CC BY 3.0/Iowa Office of the State Archaeologist; 48 ULISES RODRIGUEZ/EPA / Newscom; 49 (icon) foodonwhite / Shutterstock.com; (bottom) Indian Family in the Forest, Cornelius Krieghoff (1851), oil on canvas, Montreal Museum of Fine Arts, 1954.1105; 50-51 (corn field) ambrozinio / Shutterstock.com; 50 (inset) Aforienza / Shutterstock.com; 52 Biblioteca Digital Hispanica / Biblioteca Nacional de Espana; 53 (newspaper) Granger Historical Picture Archive / Alamy Stock Photo.

CHAPTER 5: 54-55 (landscape) Paul B. Moore / Shutterstock.com; 54 (top) Michael Hampshire / Cahokia Mounds State Historic Site; (bottom left) Sue Cunningham Photographic / Alamy Stock Photo; (bottom right) William Silver / Shutterstock.com; 56 (icon) korinoxe / Shutterstock.com; (bottom) PETER V. BIANCHI / National Geographic Creative; 57 (bottom) Sue Cunningham Photographic / Alamy Stock Photo; 58 George Burba / Shutterstock.com; 59 (top) © North Wind Picture Archives—All rights reserved; (bottom) sdart / iStockphoto.com; 60 William Silver / Shutterstock.com; (inset) magnez2 / iStockphoto.com; 61 (icon) yellowline / Shutterstock.com; 62 Reece / Shutterstock.com; 63 Michael Hampshire / Cahokia Mounds State Historic Site; 64-65 Lloyd Townsend / Cahokia Mounds State Historic Site; 65 (top) Eric Ewing / CC BY-SA 3.0.

CHAPTER 6: 67 Granger Historical Picture Archive / Alamy Stock Photo; 68 Sophia Granchinho / Shutterstock.com; 69 ZU_09 / iStockphoto.com; (icon) Firuz Salamzadeh / Shutterstock.com; 70 Edward S. Curtis Collection / Library of Congress, 40919v; 71 "Sedna and Raven" (Brazilian Soapstone) by Abraham Ruben, courtesy of Kipling Gallery; (underwater scene) Andrey_Kuzmin / Shutterstock.com; 72 (icon) Panptys / Shutterstock.com; (bottom) Robert Bird / Alamy Stock Photo; 73 Michael Rosskothen / Shutterstock.com.

CHAPTER 7: 74 Ball-play of the Choctaw—Ball Up by George Catlin (1846-1850), Smithsonian American Art Museum; 76 Stock Montage, Inc. / Alamy Stock Photo; 77 (left) Sue Stokes / Shutterstock.com; (right) Ball players, Hand-colored lithograph on paper by George Catlin (1846-1850), Smithsonian American Art Museum; 78 (cave) noreefly / Shutterstock.com; (bottom) Robert Bird / Alamy Stock Photo; 79 Granger Historical Picture Archive / Alamy Stock Photo; 81 Ball-play dance by George Catlin from Catlin's North American Indian Portfolio. Hunting Scenes and Amusements of the Rocky Mountains and Prairies of America, courtesy of Newberry Library; 82 © North Wind Picture Archives—All rights reserved; 83 © North Wind Picture Archives—All rights reserved; 84 From *Many nations: A Library of Congress resource guide for the study of Indian and Alaska native peoples of the United States*, edited by Patrick Frazier and the Publishing Office. Washington : Library of Congress, 1996, p. 57 (LC-USZC4-4807); 85 AAA Photostock / Alamy Stock Photo.

CHAPTER 8: 86 Library and Archives Canada, Acc. No. 1981-55-76 Bushnell Collection; 88-89 Michael Rosskothen / Shutterstock.com; 90 Inyea / Shutterstock.com; 91 Granger Historical Picture Archive / Alamy Stock Photo; 92 Chronicle / Alamy Stock Photo; 94-95 Library of Congress Prints and Photographs Division, LC-USZ62-44458; 97 M2-2 / Baldwin Collection / Toronto Reference Library; 98 Department Indigenous and Northern Affairs / Library and Archives Canada / e011080274; 99 (top) Saskatchewan Archives Board; (bottom) Frances Benjamin Johnston, (1864-1952) photographer / Library of Congress, 3a27591u.

CHAPTER 9: 100-101 Creative Travel Projects / Shutterstock.com; 102 Michael Wheatley / All Canada Photos; 103 Aboriginal Stock Images; 104 Design by Andrew Karpik / Legislative Assembly of Nunavut; 105 (from top to bottom) 2016 HPA / Hutchins Photo/Newscom; David Rae Morris / Polaris / Newscom; Leon Switzer / ZUMAPRESS / Newscom; Christopher Szagola / Cal Sport Media / Newscom; 106 (top left) Michael Wheatley / Alamy Stock Photo; (top right) Boomer Jerritt / All Canada Photos; 107 (top left and right) Gregory Johnston / Shutterstock.com; (bottom) BillieBonsor / Shutterstock.com; 108 Alina R / Shutterstock.com.

INDEX

adaptation 27, 29–41, 90, 103
Africa, African 16, 92
agriculture 79. *See also* crops
Alaska 17, 22, 31, 53, 66, 68, 69
Alberta 102, 107
Aleut 53
Alexie, Sherman 106
American Revolution 93
Anasazi 56, 59–61
Anishinaabe 41, 105, 106
Antiquities Act 5
Apache 92
archaeology 5, 12–13, 16, 18, 19
    context 46–47
    dating methods 12–13
    infrared technology 73
    population estimates 58
    underwater 19, 20, 21
architects, architecture 56, 59, 60
Arctic 22, 66–71, 104, 105
Arizona 56, 57, 59, 74
arrowheads 47
art 36–38, 44, 45
Asia 16, 17, 19, 25, 88
Assembly of First Nations 104
assimilation 97–99
athletes 104–5
Aztec 68

ball games 46, 48, 57
Beach, Adam 105
Beringia 14, 17, 18, 19, 21
bison. *See* buffalo
Blackfeet 107
Blackfoot 35
boarding schools. *See* residential schools
books 53
bow and arrow 39, 69–70
Britain 93, 97
British Columbia 5, 106
buffalo 33–35, 36, 41, 81, 84, 93
buildings 18, 56, 58, 60, 72. *See also* houses
Bureau of Indian Affairs 93
burial 5, 62, 64–65

Cahokia 4, 54, 61–65
California 31, 57, 92
Canada
    archaeological finds 20, 22
    Arctic Canada 104
    assimilation 97
    Atlantic Canada 53
    hockey players 105
    Indian Territories 95
    lacrosse 80
    Loyalists 96
    powwows 102, 107
    residential schools 98–99
    Truth and Reconciliation Commission 108
canals 56–58
canoes 31, 41, 44, 61, 71
caribou 36, 70, 105
carving 10, 71, 106
Catlin, George 81
cedar 10, 12, 20, 31, 32, 106
ceremony. *See also* ritual
    buffalo 34, 35
    at Cahokia 62
    ceremonial objects 46
    for 500th anniversary of Columbus 101
    Haudenosaunee 79
    Ice Age 25
    in powwows 107
    trade fairs and 84, 85
Chaco Canyon 60
Cheechoo, Jonathan 105
Cherokee 53, 96
Chickasaw 92
Choctaw 81
Christianity 88, 97
cities
    Cahokia 54, 61–65
    Pueblo Bonito 54, 60
    San Lorenzo 45–46
climate change 26–27, 36
Clovis points 47
Codex Duran 52
colonization 88–99, 102
Colorado 59
Columbus, Christopher 76, 88, 101
cooking
    fires 24, 61, 84
    lechuguilla plant 39
    whale oil 69
corn 49–51, 56, 82, 85, 103

creation myths 6–7, 10, 38, 51
Cree 74, 81, 102, 103, 105
crops 40, 56, 58, 82

dancing, dancers 25, 68, 77, 80, 83, 85
    Ghost Dance 93, 101
    powwows 102, 106–107
deserts 21, 36, 39, 56, 57
diplomacy 82
disease 58, 88, 90–91, 102
dogs 25, 37, 69
dogsleds 69

earthquakes 10, 11, 52
engineers 4, 56, 58, 60
England. *See* Britain

farmers 50, 56, 58, 84, 96
feathers 44, 53, 57
flooding 12, 17, 18, 36, 65
Florida 84, 96
food
    in Arctic 70, 71
    buffalo 33, 93
    corn 49–51
    Ice Age 23–25
    lechuguilla 39
    in Mississippi Valley 62
    pemmican 36
    trade 56, 57
    turkeys 90
    variety 76
    from Western Hemisphere 49
    wild rice 40–41
forced resettlement 89, 95–96
fossils 22, 47
Fox (tribe) 92
France 92, 93
fur trading 25, 31, 44, 56, 61, 93

Glooscap 78
grave robbing 5
Great Lakes
    harvest festivals 79
    Ice Age 21
    myths 7
    settlements 82
    slaves 92
    surrendered lands 96

wampum belts 11
    wild rice 40–41
Greenland 66, 69, 72, 73, 104
Gwitchin 22

Haida 10, 12, 32, 106
Haida Gwaii 20, 21, 28, 31
harvest 40, 50, 58, 79, 83
Haudenosaunee 6–7, 11, 74, 76, 79, 82, 105, 106
    Haudenosaunee (Iroquois) Confederacy 82, 96
Head-Smashed-In Buffalo Jump 33, 41
hockey 105
Hohokam 56, 58
Hopi 74, 80
horses 22, 27, 33, 34, 36
houses 58, 60, 61, 62, 72, 73, 76, 82
human remains 5
hunting, hunters
    after European contact 90
    archaeology and 47
    Arctic 69, 70
    buffalo 33–35
    caribou 105
    dance and 83
    Ice Age 17, 23, 24–25
    in myths 34, 41, 78, 107
    in rock art 37, 39
    seal 31, 70
    whale 31, 69

Ice Age 4, 15–27, 30, 69
    animals 16, 17, 22, 26, 27
    end of 26–27
    environment 21
    way of life 23–24
Illinois 62, 92
Indian Act (Canada) 98
Inuit 68, 70, 71, 92, 104, 105
inuksuit 105

Japan 10, 14, 19
jewelry
    Kokopelli 59
    Olmec 45, 46
    trade 56, 57, 63, 84
    turquoise 44, 60
    Viking 73

kayaks 69
Kinew, Wab 106
Kokopelli 59
Krieghoff, Cornelius 49

lacrosse 80
Lakota 98
languages 53, 77, 99, 102, 103
    sign language 44
L'Anse aux Meadows 72
lechuguilla plant 39
Lower Pecos 4, 28, 36–39, 41

mammoths 22, 27
Manhattan Island 82
Manitoba 98
Manitou 89
mastodons 22, 27, 47
Mayan 48, 51
Meadowcroft Rockshelter 14, 18
megafauna 22
Mesoamerica 44, 53
Mexico
    earliest writing 52
    San Lorenzo 45–46
    turquoise trade 60
    Yucatán 19
migration theories 16–21
Mi'kmaq 53, 74, 77, 78
Mississippian 56, 62, 65
Mississippi River 21, 61, 62, 65, 80, 95
Mississippi Valley 92
Mohawk 11, 82
Montana 107
Monte Verde, Chile 14, 18
mounds (Cahokia) 62–65
musicians 85, 105
myths 10. *See also* storytellers
    Beaver 23
    corn 51
    dancing 107
    Nanaboozhoo 41
    Sedna 71
    Sigo 78
    Sky Woman 6–7, 10
    Sun-Father 38
    Thunderbird and Whale 10, 11
    Quetzalcoatl 68
    Weasel Woman 35
    Yellow Cedar 32

Nakoda 84
National Congress of the American Indian 104
Native American Apology Resolution 108
Native American Graves Protection and
    Repatriation Act 5
Navajo 50, 96
Newfoundland 66, 72, 73, 89
New Mexico 47, 59, 96
Niro, Shelley 106
Nolan, Jordan 105
North American arrival 16–21
Nunavut 68, 104

Odjig, Daphne 41, 106
Oglala Sioux 87, 93–95
Ohio 62, 65
Ojibwa 41, 97
Oklahoma 96
Olmec 45–48, 50
Ontario 28, 40, 97, 105

Paradise Point 40, 41
Pawnee 50, 92
pemmican 33, 36, 85
Pennsylvania 18, 19, 98, 99
petroglyphs 36
pictographs 36
pigs 90
Piikani 107
Plains 33, 34, 36, 50, 62, 81, 85, 93, 107
Point, Susan 106
population
    decline 58, 91, 102
    estimates 58
    growth 82, 103
pottery 11, 13, 44, 45, 56, 57, 59, 63, 84
powwows 102, 106–107
Price, Carey 105
Pueblo 50
Pueblo Bonito 54, 60

Quebec 108

radiocarbon dating 13, 18
Raven 10, 32
Reid, Bill 10, 106
religion 97, 99
residential schools 98–99
rituals 10, 48, 50, 53, 64, 77, 80, 82. *See also* ceremony
roads 61

Robertson, Robbie 105
rock art 36–38
rubber 48, 103
Ruben, Abraham Anghik 71

Sainte-Marie, Buffy 105
salmon 31, 32, 36, 71, 76, 85
San José Mogote, Mexico 52
San Lorenzo, Mexico 42, 45, 46, 48
Saskatchewan 74, 84, 99
sculpture 46
seals 31, 70, 71
shamans 34, 38
Siberia 14, 19, 69
Sioux 87, 92–95
Sitting Bull, Chief 93
slavery 88, 89, 92
smallpox 90–91
Snaketown 54, 57, 58
South America 17, 48, 50
Southwest 50, 53, 80, 85
Spain, Spanish 53, 88–91, 92
sports 80–81
    athletes 104–5
    ball games 46, 48, 57
    double ball 81
    lacrosse 80
Starr, Emmett 53
starvation 90, 102
St. Lawrence River 21, 50, 96
storytellers, storytelling 10, 11, 77, 85, 107.
    See also myths

Tagaq, Tanya 105
tattoos 25, 61, 85
tepees 76, 87
terminology 4–5
Texas 36, 37, 39
Thule 68–69, 71, 72, 73
tools
    archaeological finds 12, 16, 18
    bone 18, 25, 31, 33
    stone 16, 18, 25, 31, 36, 103
Tootoo, Jordin 105
totem poles 12, 105
trade, traders 44, 56, 57, 61, 63, 83–85
    diseases and 90–91
Trail of Tears 96
Tribe Called Red, A 105

trickster 32, 78
Truth and Reconciliation Commission 108
tsunami 10, 11
Tuniit 69–70, 71
turquoise 44, 60

Vikings 72–73
visual artists 106

wampum belts 11
war 60, 88, 93, 102
    American War of Independence 96
    Battle of Wounded Knee 93–94
whale
    hunting 31, 69
    in mythology 10, 11, 71
wild rice 40–41
wolves 33, 34, 37, 107
Wounded Knee, Battle of 93–94
writing 52–53

Yaqui 53
Yucatán 19
Yukon 22, 23

Zuni 38, 50